Hazrat Babajan
A Pathan Sufi of Poona

Babajan, a Pathan from the Afghan territories, arrived at Poona in the early years of the twentieth century. In this British Raj city, until her death in 1931, she dwelled under a tree in the ascetic mode of a Muslim faqir. Her early life is obscure, and set against the background of nineteenth-century North India.

Hazrat Babajan: A Pathan Sufi of Poona is the only detailed and annotated work on the subject, superseding the author's early book *A Sufi Matriarch* (1986). The substance and significance of Babajan's life are recounted and assessed here. Her Sufi orientation is evident, though she was independent of the Sufi orders. The nature of this independence is investigated in a chapter on the distinctive and radical qalandar tradition. The author also addresses the topic of Sufi women over the centuries, a largely uncharted subject, which has evocative historical and social significances.

Babajan attracted many Muslim devotees, and a number of Hindu and Zoroastrian followers. Indeed, the tremendous public response to her funeral serves to prove her remarkable impact on British Raj Poona.

Hazrat Babajan sitting under the neem tree that was her final abode

Hazrat Babajan
A Pathan Sufi of Poona

Kevin R. D. Shepherd

STERLING PAPERBACKS
An imprint of
Sterling Publishers (P) Ltd.
A-59, Okhla Industrial Area, Phase-II,
New Delhi-110020.
Tel: 26387070, 26386209; Fax: 91-11-26383788
E-mail: mail@sterlingpublishers.com
www.sterlingpublishers.com

Printed in India

Printed and Published by Sterling Publishers Pvt. Ltd.,
New Delhi-110020.

Preface

$\mathcal{T}$his is a new book, incorporating some of the material in my earlier work *Hazrat Babajan: A Sufi Matriarch* (1986). That was the first book on the subject (as distinct from a booklet) and, indeed, the first annotated book.

The present work has a different format and also amplifies the content, drawing upon sources not covered in the precedent.

The name of the subject is now sometimes presented as Baba Jan. I prefer the more composite word, which is the one used in most of the sources.

I have been studying the subject for nearly fifty years, although by no means exclusively.

July 2013   **Kevin R. D. Shepherd**

Contents

1. The Background

$\mathcal{H}$azrat Babajan died in 1931. A reputed centenarian, her date of birth is uncertain. Attributions have varied from c. 1790 to c. 1830.

A major source says: "Hazrat Babajan hails from Afghanistan and was the daughter of a well-to-do Afghan of noble lineage. Her maiden name was Gul-rukh ('rose-faced'), and her early training was that befitting the status of an Afghan aristocrat." (1)

The same account, appearing eight years after her death, states a basic drawback, in that "the information gleaned from different sources is meagre, since Babajan herself was never communicative to anyone with regard to her life history." The Indian Muslim Abdul Ghani was in contact with various informants. "The facts of her early life and those relating to her spiritual career have all been confirmed by Hazrat Meher Baba, her chief disciple." (2)

A slightly earlier version came from the British writer Charles B. Purdom, who relays that "her actual date of birth is not known, but it is supposed to have been about 1790, in that land of mountains, deserts, and stony plains, Baluchistan." (3) The very early date is in query, and reference is here made to a territory adjoining Afghanistan. "Perhaps she was born on the Afghan borders near Quetta; the location is not certain." (4) The ethnic diversity in this region has caused confusion.

Baluchistan was described in early British Raj reports. Charles Masson (1800–53) was a British soldier employed by the East India Company. This explorer wrote in the early 1840s:

"Belochistan comprises the extensive regions between the confines of modern Persia and the valley of the Indus. To the north, Sistan and Afghanistan, to the south, the ocean marks its boundaries" (*Narrative of Various Journeys in Balochistan, Afghanistan, and the Punjab*, Vol 4, p. 281).

Masson investigated Eastern Baluchistan, as distinct from the Persian side; the former was included in the domain of the Khan of Kalat. The British province of Baluchistan was created during the period 1876–91, as the consequence of treaties achieved by the political agent Robert Sandeman with the Khan of Kalat. The colonial drive now gained control of Quetta and the Bolan Pass.

Quetta became the capital of the new British province, which represented an ethnic admixture ruled by the British. The Raj installed a military base at Quetta, which proved strategic in the Second Afghan War (1878–80). In earlier times, this high-altitude town had been part of the Afghan empire created by Ahmad Shah Durrani. During the 1820s, Quetta was a mud-walled fortress accompanied by simple mudbrick houses. A neighbouring zone was the Kandahar province of Afghanistan.

In 1893, Sir Mortimer Durand negotiated an agreement with the Amir of Afghanistan, making the "Durand Line" (extending from Chitral to Baluchistan) the boundary between Afghanistan and British Raj domains. This bifurcation was to cause much native resentment, surging in the Afghan (or Pathan) revolt of 1897.

Baluchistan was inhabited by the Baluch (Baloch) and Brahui peoples, who are quite distinct from Afghans. This territory extended into Iran, and was noted for barren deserts and arid plains. South of Quetta, the sparse population included Baluchi tribes living a largely nomadic and untamed existence; they combined the nomadic trait of war-like pride with elaborate codes of hospitality and honour. Some of these tribes were notorious for blood-feuds, and the men were skilled with swords. (5)

Purdom reports a discourse by Meher Baba in 1927, which informed that "Babajan was the daughter of one of the chief ministers of the Amir of Afghanistan." (6) This disclosure does not confirm an origin in Baluchistan, a territorial designation missing from the version of Ghani. A more recent report affirms that the early name of the subject was Razia Sultana. (7)

Ghani describes Gul-rukh (Babajan) as a Pathan, a detail that is ethnically important. In British colonial history, the "independent Pathan tribes" were a major component of life on the north-west frontier of India. Those Afghan tribes were part of the Afghan empire. The Pathans (or Pashtuns) were Pashtu-speakers, and the linguistic designation is now common (although one or two different ethnic groups also identify as Pashtuns). During the nineteenth century, and for much of the twentieth, the ethnic description of Pathan was generally favoured, and can still be followed.

In the struggles between rival dynasties, Pathans infiltrated the Punjab and Sind. A substantial Pathan population existed at Quetta during the nineteenth century. In the Quetta region, they existed alongside Baluchi tribes and others. The Pathans are a completely different people to the Baluch, with a separate language.

Early photographs of Pathans reveal diverse visages, often with strong profiles. Most of the images are male. Some men wore turbans, others had skull caps. A well-known photo, dating to 1921, depicts "the old Pathan," featuring a white beard and skull cap (via correspondent Maynard Owen Williams of the *National Geographic Magazine*).

Today, millions of Pathans (or Pashtuns) live in both Pakistan and Afghanistan; the vast majority of these populations are Sunni Muslims.

2. Early Life

$\mathcal{T}$ he uncertain dating for Babajan's early life requires a degree of flexibility in reporting. Her family was part of an empire aristocracy, but all details of the reign are lost. Some reference to Afghan history may be useful.

During the eighteenth century, the Afghan empire was created by Ahmad Shah Durrani (reigned 1747–72), chief of the Abdali tribe. Other Pathan tribes rallied to his cause. With 12,000 veteran Pathan warriors, this monarch invaded the Punjab and took the city of Lahore in 1748. He was afterwards defeated by the Mughal emperor Ahmad Shah (reigned 1748–54). The latter transpired to have a big problem; having been reared in a harem, the young emperor was strongly influenced by an illiterate eunuch who effectively took control, causing chaos and resentment. The Afghans became intermittent invaders, part of a situation in which various armies struggled for power and plunder. The Marathas (who were Hindus) hired mercenaries and adopted methods of European warfare; their changing mode of campaign now afflicted both Hindus and Muslims. The Mughal power declined into effete puppet rulership.

Durrani's Afghan army plundered Delhi in 1757 and 1760. They fought the Marathas, who fled from Pathan fury. The Maratha army was now accompanied by wives, camp followers, and luxury tents, quite unlike their early days of guerrilla warfare against the oppressive Mughals. They managed to capture Delhi from the Muslims, and imprisoned the ineffective Mughal emperor. Durrani's Afghan army then reappeared, cutting off Maratha supply lines and slaughtering 20,000 desperate camp followers.

The decisive battle between the Afghans and Marathas occurred at Panipat in 1761. The latter had 45,000 men, but hundreds of them are reported to have died every day of hunger and disease. Durrani had 60,000 men, and half of these included Rohillas and Mughals won over to the Pathan cause. The Muslims smashed the Maratha army, and only a quarter of that force survived. The victors enslaved the women and children. Yet by now, the Afghan troops were complaining of arrears in pay, and decided that Durrani must leave India before the stifling summer heat arrived. Durrani accordingly retreated, only to be harassed by the resilient Sikhs, who are said to have freed over 2,000 Hindu women.

These wars were ugly. Helpless villages could be annihilated or enslaved. The swords of glory dripped with blood. A Muslim warlord moved south and invaded Maharashtra with a large army. Nizam Ali destroyed Hindu temples at Toka, and lost important allies as a consequence. He nevertheless ruled the late Mughal Deccan for the next forty years.

The Islamic theologian Shah Waliullah (1703–62) was "instrumental in inviting the Afghan king Ahmad Shah Durrani Abdali to India to defend the Muslims against the Sikh and Mahratta" (Schimmel 1975, p. 372). Waliullah was active in Delhi, attempting to harmonise Islamic law with Sufism and dictating a rather insular message. "To him successful military campaigns and the process of colonisation represented an affirmation of the innate truth of Islam" (Rizvi 1983, p. 377). Shah Waliullah mistakenly believed that warlords like Durrani were the solution to social problems, and encouraged the *jihad* (holy war) concept "in order to root out polytheism" (ibid., p. 384).

In 1762, the formidable Durrani returned to North India, defeating the rival Sikh army and slaughtering many thousands. Lahore became the focus of a renewed struggle, and the Afghans eventually lost control of the Punjab to the determined Sikhs. After his invasion of 1769, Durrani had to retreat from Peshawar when his unpaid soldiers were in mutiny. His empire included Kashmir, Sind, and Baluchistan, and he ruled Afghanistan from Kabul to Kandahar.

The Afghan empire subsequently fragmented until the rise of Dost Muhammad Khan (reigned 1826–63), a Pathan of the Barakzai tribe, who ruled from Kabul. (8) The ethnic scene was diverse; the Pathans jostled with Punjabis, Baluchis, Brahuis, and other peoples.

According to Ghani, at an early age Gul-rukh became a *hafiz-i-Quran*, meaning one who learns the *Quran* by heart. (9) In addition to her native Pashtu, she learned Arabic and Persian (and subsequently Urdu). She also "developed mystical tendencies," and unlike other girls, she spent much time in solitary prayer and contemplation.

The lifestyle of Pathan aristocrats could involve travelling between camps or hill-forts (such as Quetta). Gul-rukh may have been born in a regal version of the nomadic tent. "Even the Mughal emperors at the height of their luxury had remained fond of living under cloth rather than brick, a feature reflecting their Mongol and Turkish heritage." (10)

Despite the association with Baluchistan, her family may have had some connection with a site nearer Kabul, the Afghan capital. (11) Certainly, her existence in *purdah* meant that she would have rarely glimpsed life in the outside world, from which she was effectively cloistered. Women had a totally subservient role in this society; the leaders were tribal chieftains, their warriors, and the *ulama* (clerics).

The Afghan empire featured many swordsmen. *Jihad* (holy war) often comprised a convenient pretext for attack. The role of the sword was dramatised by the distinctive martial dance known as *khattak* (primarily associated with the Khattak tribe), usually performed by clans before conflict with the enemy.

"Forming a circle, sometimes every warrior holding a sword in each hand, they would follow a prescribed and rapid course of movement to the rhythmic beat of drum and tambourine. Energetic sword-thrusts at various sweeping angles were combined with personal agility to present a dramatic exhibition of poise and fury besides which the later Hollywood imitations were sedate ballet dances... real blood was often spilt between allied clans even during these preliminaries." (12)

Some dervish groups assimilated sword rituals. One description relates to enthusiasts who marched in a circle, inflicting wounds upon themselves with swords and knives. "They would even handle red-hot weapons and place them between their teeth, in the inveterate warrior (*ghazi*) spirit of immunity to trifling physical discomforts." (13)

As she grew up, Gul-rukh was probably averse to swords. She could see them everywhere, often accompanied by sharp daggers. Some men had belts stuffed with weapons, including pistols acquired/copied from Europeans. Pathan warriors could fight like berserkers, taking sword cuts until these became lethal. The *ulama* also lived by the sword, but exhorting to the Quranic *jihad* rather than wielding weapons themselves. Gul-rukh eventually came into conflict with the *ulama*.

3. Pathans and the British

The Pathan tribes depended on agriculture for livelihood. They nurtured strong egalitarian tendencies, which to some extent tempered the role of chieftains. Yet they became notorious for feuds, making unity difficult. Probably the most well-known Pathan grouping was the Afridi tribe; these hill warriors gained a reputation as formidable fighters from Mughal times, and guarded the strategic Khyber Pass.

In 1672 the Afridis gained a new ruler in Akmal Khan, who took control of the Khyber Pass in a revolt against the Mughal emperor Aurangzeb. The Afridi warriors then massacred a Mughal army between Peshawar and Kabul. Another Mughal army was repelled the following year. The grim Aurangzeb resolved to personally lead a further campaign in 1674, which was more successful. However, the emperor was obliged to offer rewards to the Pathan chieftains in order to protect the vital trade route. In this arrangement, the chieftains were paid for service to the Mughals, a measure which restored peace for twenty years.

When the British gained a strong foothold in India during the eighteenth century, competition with the French was accompanied by a new infantry armed with muskets and bayonets. The violent Afghan empire of Ahmad Shah Durrani (d. 1772) was not secure, and fell into a power vacuum in North India, at first filled by diverse adventurers and the Sikhs.

The British army initially underestimated the Pathans. In 1842, the First Afghan War resulted in a severe defeat for the colonialists serving Queen Victoria. The Pathans massacred a column of 16,000 who retreated from Kabul down the Gandamak Pass. The dead were mainly Indian troops and civilian camp followers. There was only one survivor. The Pathans had proved that the British Empire was not invincible.

In 1842, Gul-rukh may still have been young, or perhaps older if Ghani's assessment is credited that she lived to the age of 125. This is too much of a round figure for sceptics, who might credit about twenty years less. If one assigns her early life to the reign of Dost Muhammad Khan, who became the Afghan ruler in 1826, this was still a vintage era with considerable colour for any historian.

In 1879, the British gained control of the Khyber Pass, the all-important avenue to and from Kabul. The Afghan people also faced an associated problem. After 1880, the new *amir* (ruler) Abdur Rahman Khan (reigned 1880–1901) ruthlessly eliminated the Pathan system of tribal and regional autonomy. "When faced with numerous revolts by his own relatives and regional groups, he waged war against his own people until he and his government had no rivals of any type." (14) The repercussions ultimately led to a civil war in 1929. Meanwhile, the British interests were in strong evidence.

Sir Winston Churchill (1874–1965) was a participant in quelling the Pathan revolt of 1897. He was then a young lieutenant, and also a journalist for the *Daily Telegraph* in London. His despatches were very much in the British Raj spirit, and likewise his book *Story of the Malakand Field Force: An Episode of Frontier War* (1898). Churchill viewed the Pathans as aboriginal savages incited to fanaticism by their religion. The presence of the British army in such remote locations was thereby conveniently justified.

The *mullas* (religious teachers) did indeed incite tribes to *jihad* (holy war). However, the Pathans had legitimate grievances such as an imposed tax on salt, the movement of British troops in their territory, and the bisection of tribal lands. The native resentment at the official separation of India from Afghanistan caused an attack upon the British garrison at Malakand. The siege was instigated by a militant Pathan *faqir* (ascetic) known as Saidullah, an orthodox preacher who claimed miraculous powers.

The British retaliation destroyed Pathan villages, and adjacent forts were blown up with dynamite. Crops were burnt. The Pathans met with heavy casualties, caused by the lethal repeating rifles of the British force. Soon after, fines were imposed upon the surviving Afridi tribesmen, who surrendered their inferior rifles. Malakand subsequently became part of the North-West Frontier Province, innovated in 1901 by the British Raj, who were now swallowing up Afghan territories. This new province was earlier a part of the Afghan empire, and included the key city of Peshawar, gateway to the Khyber Pass.

Gul-rukh also became a *faqir*, but of a very different type to the *jihad* activists. The political friction between Afghans and the British is not irrelevant to her position, as she is reported (by Ghani) to have been living in the North-West Frontier Province, a reference apparently signifying the very early years of the twentieth century, at a time when she suffered the hostile attention of Islamic religious orthodoxy.

4. Peshawar and Rawalpindi

*G*ul-rukh was reared under the *purdah* system, in which women were secluded from the outside world. Female education could not go very far, being subservient to the system of arranged marriages and patriarchal clericalism. A marriage was planned for her, to which she was averse. She preferred solitary contemplation. According to the basic report, she ran away from home on her wedding day, at the age of eighteen.

Adjusting to the changed environment could not have been easy. It is not known exactly how she did this. Bandits abounded, and they could easily take slaves. Losing aristocratic identity, Gul-rukh made her way to Peshawar, the frontier city at the foot of the Khyber Pass. Some have believed that she was fleeing from Baluchistan, but her destination would suggest that she came from Kabul, which was much nearer. Kabul had been the Afghan capital since 1776. Peshawar was used as the "winter capital" by the Afghan rulers until the Sikhs gained power there in 1818, led by the formidable Ranjit Singh, who became ruler of the Punjab, an extensive province with urban centres like Lahore.

Nothing is known of what Gul-rukh did at Peshawar. Instead, we know that the Afghan ruler Dost Muhammad Khan tried to wrest that city from the Sikhs in 1835. He found that his Pathan army refused to fight the Sikhs, who had become a strong military force, involving "a highly trained army on western lines, partly officered by Europeans, and backed by a powerful artillery." (15) The Sikhs themselves

were a religious minority, formerly repressed by the
Mughals; they emerged from their hill forts when Mughal
rule declined in the Punjab. The Sikh general Ranjit Singh
extensively employed both Hindus and Muslims, reflecting a
prudent tolerance; he has been viewed as a provincial version
of Akbar. Peshawar remained under Sikh control until the
British took the city in 1849, ending the Sikh empire.

Gul-rukh subsequently moved to Rawalpindi, a city of
the Punjab about a hundred miles east. In or near that city,
she lived "an ascetic life for some years" (Ghani 1939, p. 32).
She had commenced the role of *faqiri* ("poverty"), associated
with Sufism. Yet no formal code of observance is implied.
Indeed, the account of Ghani informs that "a Hindu saint"
guided her into the spiritual path. The identity of this person
escaped reporting.

Afterwards, the female ascetic (*faqir*) went into seclusion
at a nearby mountain outside Rawalpindi. For nearly
seventeen months, she undertook severe austerities (*riyaz*),
but no further details are available.

One assertion has been that Babajan moved to Rawalpindi
circa 1860. This rather awkward dating is purportedly derived
from "biographical tradition" which describes her "staying in
Peshawar before moving to the garrison town of Rawalpindi
a decade or so after its foundation in 1849" (Green 2009, p.
128). The problem being that the biographical tradition (of
Ghani, Purdom, and others) makes no such chronological
calculation.

The date is totally elusive. We know that the old city of
Rawalpindi was taken by Ranjit Singh in 1818. The British
invaded this zone in 1849, and the city thereafter harboured a
permanent British garrison, eventually becoming the biggest
cantonment in India by the turn of the century. Babajan may
have arrived before the British did. It is not known whether
she lived in the British cantonment at any time.

5. *Fana-Baqa* Complexity

$\mathcal{F}$rom Rawalpindi, Gul-rukh moved south to Multan, another city in the Punjab. She was now thirty-seven years old. Here she encountered a Muslim saint, whom one commentator has identified as Maula Shah. (16) Yet no name is supplied in the early report of Ghani, who describes this Sufi as a *majzub*, a term which has been given different meanings, and which was generally used very loosely in India. Ghani employed this term in the idealistic sense of being "immersed in divinity," to cite his own phrase. The obscure entity "put an end to her spiritual struggle by giving her God-Realization." (17)

After staying a few months in Multan, she returned to Rawalpindi, where she recontacted the Hindu saint. Ghani describes the consequence in terms of: "the [Hindu] saint helps her to come down from the superconscious state of God-realization to the normal consciousness." The duration of time involved here is not specified.

These events gained an extension in literature via the reporting of Charles Purdom. He narrated a discourse given by Meher Baba in 1927, which made reference to Babajan. "After long wanderings she at last came across her [spiritual] master, and was God-realized at the age of sixty-five." (18) In a later work, Purdom relayed: "After years in search of God she found a Master, who many years afterwards (at the age of sixty-five, it is said) made her perfect." (19)

Many critics of such themes have difficulty in crediting, or fathoming, the significances. One option is to follow through the details as they stand. An obvious factor is that the Purdom references appear to contradict the report of Ghani. A solution is to infer that the process of stabilising consciousness was more protracted than is indicated in the latter report. "This would mean that twenty-eight years had elapsed since her achievement of *fana* at Multan" (Shepherd 1986, p. 39). I was here referring to the *fana-baqa* transition mentioned in Sufi teaching. *Baqa* (or *baqa-billah*) "is fundamentally an objectivising process," (20) involving a return to "normal consciousness."

It is relevant to emphasise that Babajan herself had no interest in describing her early life. She had to be pressed for details, which were not easily forthcoming. She was definitely not a promotionalist.

The occurrence of mystical teachings in widespread formats can lead to the question of which is the most applicable. The concept of a return to normal consciousness is often neglected. Sufism is made more difficult to some Western readers because of the extensive number of unfamiliar words in other languages, meaning Persian and Arabic. Some of these words can be found with different significations and interpretations attached to them, including rather dogmatic insistences. There were varying types of Sufi exponent, and different lifestyles represented. There are pronounced complexities involved, which are nevertheless frequently simplified.

6. Sir Richard Burton and Sufis of Sind

A complement to Chapter Five is applicable here to illustrate the variegated nature of "Sufism." During the late 1840s, the British soldier Captain Richard F. Burton (1821–1890) made some investigations in Sind, an adjoining province to the Punjab. He expressed respect for Pathans, many of whom had settled in Sind, and some of whom could speak four or five languages. "In appearance they are a large and uncommonly handsome race of people, perfectly distinct from the common Sindhis" (Burton 1851, p. 234).

Burton was an officer in the Bombay army of the East India Company. He was also an ethnographer, linguist, and explorer. He studied Sufism, and adopted observances of fasting and prayer; he emerges as an unusual partisan. His well-known book on Sind has a chapter entitled "On *Tasawwuf, or Sufyism, in Sindh.*" Some of the terminology he used now appears idiosyncratic, and certain components of his reporting may reflect garbled sources, but a number of details nevertheless require attention.

Burton awards deference to Sufi idealism, but is also critical of aberrations. He refers to a category of Sufi known as *salik-i majzub*, who continue to observe all the external practices of Islam. A contrasting category was known as *majzub-i salik*, reputed to be effectively dead to excitement, hope, and fear. "This class is of course rare, and requires a peculiar conformation of mind. The pretenders to it are common in proportion as the pretence is easy and its advantages great." These pretenders are described in terms of "a professed debauchee, and a successful beggar."

The commentator also describes the radical *majzub* category in terms of a freethinker explaining away "the necessity of all rites such as ablution, prayer, fasting, and fight for the faith," here meaning *jihad*. In this respect, the *majzub* is said to resemble the *hukama* or philosophers, who were not bound to belief in the *Quran* (Burton 1851, pp. 218–19).

Burton reports that between fifty and sixty *pirs* (Sufi leaders) existed in Sind, most of whom could trace their genealogies to the Prophet Muhammad. "Under our [British] government, they have lost the right of flogging and beheading their followers, so that their power now depends principally upon the ignorance and superstition of the populace." The British critic says that there were probably more than a hundred other saints of lesser standing.

According to Burton, "the Pir who calls himself a Fakir, or beggar, will probably maintain an establishment of a hundred servants, and as many horses." Furthermore, those *pirs* levied "a tax of from one-eighth to one-half upon the income and produce" of their followers (Burton 1851, pp. 204, 206).

The Sufi *pirs* in Sind were landowners, a status shared by many leaders in the established Sufi orders. The claim to be a *faqir* was discrepant with the example of rigorous ascetics associated with the same popular designation, entities who were often less visible, leading a very different lifestyle. The *pirs* gained a sense of importance from their Sufi pedigrees, frequently hereditary, which went back generations to claim famous celebrities.

In the *pir* context, Burton mentions the four major Sufi (or dervish) orders in India (Qadiri, Naqshbandi, Chishti, and Suhrawardi), and informs that the Qadiriyya and Naqshbandiyya were the most common in Sind. These four organisations had exercised a strong influence upon popular Indian Sufism, and continued to do so.

The British investigator became officially ordained as a "master Sufi." His affiliation was to the Qadiri order. However, he was scathingly critical of the pretenders, and implies that many *pirs* were charlatans, luring gullible disciples. (21)

In his account of Sind, Burton referred to the local saint worship in which women figured. There were many legends in that province about female saints. He referred to the *faqirani* (female *faqir*), a category who "occasionally rise to the high rank of a *murshid*" (Burton 1851, p. 231; cf. Schimmel 1975, p. 433-4). The Arabic word *murshid* denotes a Sufi teacher, and is an equivalent to the Persian word *pir*. The *faqirani* generally survived only in legend and miracle stories.

According to Burton, a contemporary female Naqshbandi affiliate known as Nur Bai lived in great pomp, although scandalous reports of her private life were in evidence. The British reporter says that every celebrated male *murshid* in Sind had a number of female ascetics in his periphery; these women were "married and unmarried, Hindoos as well as Moslems." The women, especially the widows, wore green clothes and carried a large rosary. Burton implies that promiscuity was a tendency in these circles, which he apparently associated with imitators in the spurious *majzub* category.

Babajan was not one of the *pirs*, and had no known affiliation with any Sufi order. She did not trace any genealogy, not claiming any *silsila* (lineage). She had renounced the landowner lifestyle attended by servants and chattels. Babajan did not remain near a male teacher, and became a very independent *faqirani*, quite separate from sectarian groupings. She was not antinomian in her approach. She did not wear green clothes, nor any form of regulation apparel, and is not known to have carried a rosary. In deference to her insistence upon a masculine role, I will use the word *faqir*, as distinct from *faqirani*, to describe the subject.

7. Journeys and Mecca

At some unknown date, Babajan commenced "a long trail of journeys from one part of India to another." Ghani relates that she visited Bombay on one of these journeys, but after only a few months in this metropolis, she returned again to the Punjab, thereafter living "a good number of years at different places in Northern India."

She reputedly travelled to Mecca disguised as a man, taking the difficult overland route from Afghanistan to Turkey, and then travelling south via Syria and Lebanon. At the Ka'bah shrine in Mecca, she is said to have offered the customary Islamic prayers. In Mecca "she would often gather food for the poor, and personally nursed pilgrims who had fallen ill." (22) She also visited the tomb of the Prophet Muhammad at Medina. In addition, she may have visited the famous tomb of Abdul Qadir Jilani at Baghdad, much favoured by Indian Muslims. However, the legends concerned are not reliable.

These details are not found in the accounts of Ghani, who nevertheless does inform that Babajan voyaged to Mecca and Medina in 1903. Ghani supplies an anecdote originating from Professor Hyder Ibrahim Sayani, who taught at the Deccan College. Sayani travelled on the steamer S.S. Hyderi, and recounted a "miracle" of how Babajan saved the ship from a cyclonic wind; via the intermediary Nur Muhammad Pankhawala, she asked all the passengers to offer a prayer. (23) The Meccan pilgrimage was prone to elaborations in hagiology. However, it is obvious enough that Babajan did travel to the Hejaz that year.

The preceding year (1902), the Wahhabis had captured the fortress town of Riyadh, and later established the new kingdom of Saudi Arabia. The fundamentalist Wahhabi regime of Abdul Aziz ibn Saud also eliminated the paraphernalia of dervish orders (i.e. Sufi orders) in the Meccan zone. An irony is that the puritans would have found very little to contradict in the case of Babajan, who "gave no 'initiations,' no *zikr* (chant), no set teachings, professed no affiliation with any organisation, emphasised no externals of practice whatsoever." (24)

Although Babajan has been classified as a Sufi, she was not typical of popular conceptions, and was substantially removed from the "dervish order" approach.

8. Burial Alive and the Baluch Regiment

*I*n the Punjab during the late nineteenth century, Babajan gained some fame as a saint. She also aroused extreme opposition from orthodox Muslims after uttering ecstatic words denoting an identity with the divine. The mystical reverie was considered blasphemous. Local *ulama* (religious teachers) were apparently at the root of this aversion. Yet the active party were reputedly *sepoys* (soldiers), and more specifically, Baluchis of a local battalion.

According to an early report, the Baluchi soldiers believed Babajan to be a heretic, and one night they vengefully buried her alive. Resort to premature burial in that zone has been interpreted in terms of a persisting tribal custom. Extremist censure could certainly result from nonconformist traits in Islamic society. Women had a low status in that society, and were not generally so visible as Babajan. How she escaped the severe predicament is not known.

Years later, the same soldiers were startled to find their victim sitting under a tree at the British cantonment in Poona, far to the south. According to Ghani:

> "The Baluchi sepoys looked upon this as a great miracle, and thus feeling convinced of her spiritual greatness, gave Gul-rukh an ovation by bowing to her reverentially. After this incident, her saintly fame spread far and wide, and she came to be universally known as Hazrat Babajan." (25)

This event at Poona has been dated to 1914, (26) when these members of a Baluch Regiment were en route to the Near East for action in the First World War. Some of these men are said to have become devotees of the matriarch, thereafter zealously protecting her as bodyguards in their off duty hours. The respectful term *Hazrat* was frequently used to designate Muslim saints.

A critical commentary has stated: "It is impossible to assess the historicity of Baba Jan's live burial" (Green 2009, p. 130). An accompanying assertion is that the incident "was scarcely original," meaning stories of live burial were a common theme and practice among Muslim and Hindu ascetics in India. However, this approach tends to be ridiculously evasive of the real significance of the burial alive. A Muslim woman was interred against her will by rabid fundamentalists. This was not at all the same scenario as self-instigated rigours on the part of male ascetics, who were acting of their own freewill, and too often in the manner of a stunt.

The burial alive probably did actually happen. Realistically, the episode fits a pattern of severe orthodox religious stricture in that part of the globe; as is well known today, homosexuals and marginalised religious orientation can receive harsh censure in the milieu here discussed. Babajan may conceivably have escaped soon after the ordeal, with the assistance of sympathisers on the same night. Rescue might have been easier to achieve if the victim was interred in a vault or existing tomb, for the convenience of nocturnal aggressors. In that event, she would not have been dead, but in sore danger of expiry.

The Baluchi soldiers are a complex subject of military history. In 1840, a British officer described the Baluchis as the best swordsmen in the world (cf. Burton 1851, p. 240, who says the Baluchi "is a bold and strong, but by no means a skilful swordsman, utterly ignorant of the thrust"). When the British annexed the province of Sind, after defeating a confederacy of Baluchi chieftains in that zone, the Baluchi warriors were in demand as army soldiers. General Sir Charles Napier was impressed with their fighting spirit and reckless courage, and wished to assimilate them into British ranks. The "Bellochee Battalion" of 1844 was mostly recruited from Baluchis, Sindis, and Pathans from Sind.

The Baluchi *sepoys* assimilated the new rifle power that made the sword comparatively obsolete. They became celebrated for a high standard of performance. In the early years of their formation, several battalions were created. By 1901, all of these became Baluch Regiments. All five Regiments were in active service during the Great War of 1914–18, the locations varying from Eastern countries to the Western Front. In 1914, a member of the Regiment active in France became the first Indian soldier (namely Khudadad Khan) to be awarded the Victoria Cross. (27)

9. Poona and the British Raj

$\mathcal{B}$abajan settled in Poona by 1905, and was to remain in that city for the rest of her life. During the British Empire era and later, the place-name was rendered as Poona, not Pune, which is more familiar today. I will follow the name found in the sources.

Poona was located in the Deccan, another name no longer visible on maps. A popular name for this city became "Queen of the Deccan." Poona was a centre of the British Raj, which maintained a large cantonment there. By comparison with the turbulent Punjab, the Deccan had a relaxed atmosphere. Poona enjoyed mild summers, due to the high altitude of some 1800 feet above sea level. It was just over a hundred miles from Bombay (Mumbai), being closely linked with the British administration at the metropolis.

The cantonment adjoined the old city, which was divided into *peths* or zones, such as Kasba Peth. The word *peth* is Marathi. Some of these zones dated to the early British rule, and others from former times, meaning the Maratha empire and the preceding period of Mughal annexation in the seventeenth century. A number of *peths* originally had Islamic names, but these were altered in 1791. Before the Mughals, the Sultans of Ahmednagar had been the rulers.

Poona had a strong Hindu majority, with the Muslims being a minority. There were smaller populations of Christians, Jains, and Zoroastrians. Many Hindu temples were in evidence, reflecting the former salience of the city as a capital of the Maratha Empire. From here, the Maratha

ruler known as the Peshwa had controlled the province of
Maharashtra during the eighteenth century. After martially
competing with the Afghans in the north, the Peshwa lost
his territories to the insatiable British feat of annexation, and
was silenced with an adroit pension. From 1818 onwards,
the Anglo-Saxon administrators of Bombay were kings of
the peninsula. This phase is sometimes known in the history
books as British hegemony.

In the Punjab, Babajan would have often glimpsed the
British overlords, if from a distance. Now she was moving
into a major centre of the Raj (British rule), where decorum
was immaculate, and where power was both military and
economic. In 1858, British Crown rule had been imposed in
India as a bulwark against the Indian Mutiny of that period.

Neither the Hindu rulership nor the British Raj assisted
the people at large. Many untouchables still existed in the
villages of Maharashtra, condemned to ignominy and stigma.
The Governor General of Bombay, like the Peshwa before
him, lived in opulence and comfort. The poor suffered dirt,
malnutrition, disease, and lack of education.

Babajan lived on the level of the poor, her extremely simple
lifestyle demonstrating a high ideal of *faqiri* ("poverty"). No
property, no possessions, no status. The British social elite
were in revulsion at such an existence. In similar contrast
were the wealthy Hindu priests and the wealthy Muslim
ulama. Renunciation of status remains a basic qualification for
a way of life that may differ in expression, but not in essential
content. The word renunciation is, of course, anathema to the
wealthy status elites of royalty, politics, academe, religious
office, big business, and entertainment showbiz. However,
academe will sometimes profile discrepancies in status roles.

One of the more useful BBC articles (dating to 2011)
has remarked on several factors involved in the British Raj
phenomenon, which can be summarised as follows:

The British criticised the social divisions visible in the Hindu caste system, but their own lifestyle was riddled with class biases and precedence complexes. Even the "Anglo-Indians" were racially inferior, in this elitist perspective.

"Successive viceroys in India and secretaries of state in London were appointed on a party basis, having little or no direct experience of Indian conditions." The first serving British secretary of state (Edwin Montagu) to visit India, on a mission to find facts, made his appearance in that country in 1917-18, decidedly late in the day, and far too late in realistic terms.

India provided Britain with two undisputed economic benefits. This means that India "was a captive market for British goods and services, and served defence needs by maintaining a large standing army at no cost to the British taxpayer."

National benefits for India, created by the British Raj, included railways, canals, shipping, and mining. Also listed in this context are the creation of an education system in English, law and order, and integration into a world economy.

Drawbacks of the Raj have been emphasised in terms of "leaving Indians poorer and more prone to devastating famines, exhorting high taxation in cash from an impecunious people... draining Indian revenues to pay for an expensive bureaucracy (including in London) and an army beyond India's own defence needs; servicing a huge sterling debt, not ensuring that the returns from capital investment were reinvested to develop the Indian economy rather than reimbursed to London; and retaining the levers of economic power in British hands." (28)

10. Amma Saheb alias Hazrat Babajan

*B*abajan never wore a veil, and always described herself as a man. She would respond negatively to the name of *Mai*, meaning "mother." She would retort, "I am a man and not a woman." (29) She can be interpreted as insisting upon equality with those who dominated society. Muslims often called her Amma ("Mother") Saheb, representing a combination of genders. The word *saheb* was a term of respect for Indians of rank, and also European gentlemen; the meaning is approximately Sir. The feminine application is *saheba*.

However, the name Babajan was the ultimate victor. Different interpretations have been given to this name, which has been described as "a man's name" (Burman 2002, p. 237). This appellation is by no means unique to the Sufi matriarch of Poona.

The name Babajan has been defined by some analysts in terms of derivation from the Turkish *baba*, meaning "father," and the Persian *jan*, meaning approximately "dear one." The word *baba* originally applied to Turkish religious leaders of the Anatolian phase, and acquired a widespread use in India, being frequently applied to Sufis, and gaining the sense of a wise old man. The word *baba* was also assimilated by Hinduism, being used as a title of respect for some Hindu holy men, e.g. Upasni Baba (alias Maharaj) of Sakori, a contemporary of Babajan.

The same word *baba* also has an element of ambiguity, passing through different languages, and acquiring another meaning of "child." Babajan herself is reported to have used the term *baba* in the junior context when referring to devotees and others (Ghani 1939, p. 35). Her own name should be distinguished from this more common usage.

One interpretation describes the name Babajan as "a nickname based on the term of endearment for a 'dear child' (*baba jan*) that echoes Bane Miyan's own childlike moniker" (Green 2009, p. 128). The preoccupation here with Bane Miyan (a distant male contemporary) appears to have contracted the significances. Babajan called everyone "child," and asserted herself as a man in the face of a chronic social and religious inequality. In her case, the equivocal word *baba* was considered by her followers to possess a masculine quality. Her well-known disciple Merwan Irani (Meher Baba) even made the benign gesture of calling her the "old man", which received her approval. He did not call her the dear child, which would have been an insult.

Her devotees appear to have employed the name Babajan in a respectful context of authority, and also deferring to the masculine identity preference of the matriarch. In this respect, "dear Father" is the relevant translation. Some have treated *jan* as a Sufi term meaning soul or spirit, and in this more extended linguistic subtlety, the name Babajan becomes "Father soul."

11. Early Days in Poona

At first, Babajan had no fixed place of abode in Poona. Instead, she moved between different parts of the city and cantonment, including the abject slum areas, contrasting with the affluent homes of British residents. Her lifestyle was that of a street mendicant; she did not stay in houses or hostels. She had apparently been living in this manner for much of her adult life, ever since she forsook her aristocratic *purdah*. However, her tendency was to stay at specific sites.

Amma Saheb, alias Hazrat Babajan, had developed a high degree of resistance to discomforts. During her early days in Poona, she stayed at one period near the Muslim shrine of Panch Pir at Dighi. This vicinity was plagued with ants, and a Muslim devotee discovered that Babajan was covered with these insects and suffering their bites without qualm. The concerned visitor was Kasim Rafai, one of her early followers in Poona. He obtained her permission to remove the ants, but was not successful. With some difficulty, he then persuaded her to visit his house, where his family laboriously removed hundreds of the troublesome insects from her person. (30)

A basic feature of Babajan's career was her explicit commitment to *faqiri*, a term of Arabic origin, and denoting the ascetic lifestyle associated with Sufis. In conformity with that ideal, she had no home and no possessions. This was not the helpless poverty of the Indian masses, but a deliberate choice made in pursuit of a spiritual objective. When devotees gifted her with presents, she would give these away to the poor, who were never far away, even in British Poona. Her only belongings were the clothes she wore, which did not fit any standard ascetic apparel of Sufis.

There are some similarities with her contemporary Sai Baba of Shirdi (d. 1918), another Sufi *faqir*, and one who lived in a dilapidated rural mosque that was comfortable by comparison with her own situation. Even Shirdi Sai (31) was not as hardy as Babajan, being afflicted by an asthmatic tendency; the matriarch was remarkably robust and of a more advanced age.

The "outdoor poverty" role of Hazrat Babajan serves to distinguish her from the commercial saints and gurus who gained such attention from *circa* 1970 onwards, including the notorious entity at Poona who selfishly invested in a large fleet of expensive Rolls Royce automobiles.

Dr. Ghani left the following description of Babajan, whom he knew at first-hand during her last years:

"Short in stature, firm and agile in gait, back slightly bent with rounded shoulders, skin fair and sunburnt, face broad and heavily wrinkled, high cheek bones, liquid blue eyes possessing great depths, head covered with a silvery crown of thick white hair hanging loose to the shoulders, deep sonorous voice, all conspired to make her personality very unique and unworldly. Her attire was simple, consisting of a long apron extending below the knees, a pyjamas [*paejamah*, or trousers] narrowed round the legs and a linen scarf thrown carelessly round the shoulders. She always went about bare-headed; the luxuriant crop of white hair – never oiled or groomed – was for all practical purposes a headdress in itself." (32)

Some Tibetan Buddhist nuns had more elaborate coiffures of thick (black) hair that have been deemed startling in nineteenth century photography. However, those Mahayana nuns were part of a cordoning and protective monastic system, and did not integrate with mundane and public circumstances like Babajan.

A basic detail about the subject is that she was nothing of a preacher. She did not talk about *jihad*, hellfire, or other favoured subjects of zealots. Nor did she depend upon associations with Sufi orders and prestigious pedigrees. It is the differences, not any similarities, that are remarkable in her case.

12. Rasta Peth and Muslim Devotees

At Poona, Babajan eventually settled under a *neem* tree near the mosque of Bukhari Shah in Rasta Peth suburb. (33) Close by was the home of Sardar Raste, a Muslim who had become her devotee. Little is known about this man, but there was already an early group of Poona devotees, including Kasim Rafai. They assisted Babajan in whatever way they could, and were keen for her to visit their homes, which they considered a blessing, if she was willing to do so.

Another Muslim devotee was Shaikh Imam, a watchmaker by profession, who lived in the cantonment. Babajan often visited his home in her early years at Poona (and probably much later). His mother was also a devotee, and is reported to have given Babajan a bath. Certain sources say that Babajan did not bathe during her last years, but this assumption has been contested as amounting to a miracle story. Her immediate living space was not convenient to privacy, and private houses were the solution for purposes of washing. (34)

Crowds began to assemble near the mosque, and there was little space. Devotees requested Babajan to choose another site for visitor convenience, but she refused. The matriarch only moved when a large banyan tree nearby was chopped down to make the road wider. It is evident that she preferred trees to municipal developments, which were basically concerned with the new motor traffic favoured by the British.

The Rasta Peth phase served to form the nucleus of Babajan's substantial later following in Poona. The devotees found in her an unusual specimen of the *faqir* lifestyle; she was not a formalist Sufi, and existed in complete simplicity.

An eyewitness described her as "a perfect embodiment of resignation and self-abnegation (*tasleem-o-raza*)" (Ghani 1939, p. 34). Such qualities would run the risk today of being considered a mere fatalism by the glib sceptics who abound. What Babajan did was not meditation but something else. There was no closed eyes pose, and no chant.

13. Living under a Neem Tree at Char Bavadi

*T*he matriarch now stayed for a short period near a deserted tomb in the Swar Gate locality. Then she moved to another *neem* tree, this time in the Char Bavadi vicinity, and on the fringe of the British cantonment. Ghani refers to the place as Malcolm Tank. Only after some months did she permit her Muslim devotees to erect a simple shelter made of sacking (the common gunny cloth). Here she stayed for the rest of her life, meaning over twenty years.

Babajan apparently selected Char Bavadi because some devotees lived nearby. Also, she may already have been in contact with a number of Pathan soldiers at the cantonment barracks. Yet the new site was at first extremely unaccommodating. The dirt road was notorious for mosquitoes. Babajan was habitually indifferent to irritations.

In this area, there were also nocturnal gatherings of drunkards, thieves, and drug addicts. The devotees were concerned about these loiterers, some of whom were considered to be dangerous. However, Babajan herself did not discriminate against low-class people, even if they were non-Muslims. The nocturnal "riff-raff" (as Dr. Ghani called them) were low-class Hindus, and mainly petty thieves and pickpockets who liked to drink toddy (palm wine) when they could pay for it. They would drink to excess. An unspecified number of the "riff-raff" were drug addicts, opting for cannabis and opium. At that time, cannabis was commonly smoked by labourers in Indian society (and usually admixed with tobacco).

Babajan was estranged from the nocturnal pursuits. At some point, the devotees elected an attendant (*mujawar*) to protect her and see to her needs. The Muslim matriarch was tolerant of Hindus, but would never allow the customary *darshan* prostration which Hindus anticipated when meeting saints or holy persons. The "riff-raff" treated her with respect, and even adulation. However, some of them were opportunistic. They soon grasped that Babajan was occasionally given presents by devotees, but that she did not really want these things, being a renouncing *faqir*. They also discovered that if one or two of them could steal the gifts from her, she was lenient towards the miscreants.

This situation led to dramas in which the "riff-raff" were opposed by devotees. After a few years, the problem of bad behaviour at Char Bavadi was virtually eliminated by a strong contingent of Muslim soldier devotees, who could be very disapproving of Hindu transgressions.

The soldiers (*sepoys*) came from the nearby barracks. These were Pathans, and later also Baluchis. The Pathans quickly became loyal followers of Babajan. When they were present, most Hindus dared not get too close. In their off-duty hours, the *sepoys* tended to form a bodyguard at the *neem* tree. This development, *circa* 1910, apparently originated in an objection to the local underworld of thieves and drug addicts, who would steal from Babajan and devotees. The *sepoys* were a strong deterrent to the "riff-raff," who gravitated elsewhere, fearful of being berated and punished by sturdy Pathans.

Some readers have been confused by descriptions of this period. It has even been imagined that a den of drug addicts frequented the *neem* tree, in close intimacy with Babajan. The reality was quite different. To start with, different religious backgrounds were involved. The "haunt" was not at the tree, but along the street. Most of the "riff-raff" do not appear to have been residents, but rather interlopers, seeking to escape police attention in a relatively unfrequented locale. The street featured dilapidated slum buildings and dingy oil lamps, like many other low-class streets in Poona.

The standpoint of Babajan was that drugs and medical treatments amounted to a reduction and disqualification of *faqiri*, the *faqir* lifestyle. In other words, the true *faqir* does not resort to artificial highs and dependence on European palliatives.

Many Hindus were afraid of Pathan soldiers, who could be fierce in confrontation with "infidels" (*kafirs*), and who were in contact with the police. Drunkards had no chance against them. Drugs were not at that time prohibited, but theft was, and suspect loitering tendencies of roughnecks could be strongly addressed.

Within a decade, there were further changes at the *neem* tree. "The locality underwent a metamorphosis surpassing all expectations." Char Bavadi became "a place of pilgrimage for people from all over India." (35)

"The squalid slum area gained a prosperous facelift.... This was not due to any city council or cantonment project, but because of the matriarch under the tree. The flow of visitors gained pilgrimage overtones, and to an extent that the Char Bavadi vicinity gained a popularity amongst shopkeepers. New buildings sprang up, and old ones were renovated. Teashops did a thriving trade, their customers taking welcome refreshment while waiting to see Babajan." (36)

Some large new buildings were constructed, and electricity appeared in local homes (a sign of affluence at that time). As a direct consequence of Babajan's appearance under the *neem* tree, Char Bavadi "became a charming area in which to live and raise a family" (Kalchuri 1986, p. 14). Some of her middle-class Muslim devotees appear to have moved into the locality. This would help to explain the new money that was poured into the local environment.

At first, thieves occasionally managed to breach the guard
provided by soldiers and devotees. One crafty loiterer stole a
shawl from Babajan while she lay resting, and another man
roughly snatched two gold bangles from her wrists, drawing
blood. However, Babajan expressed annoyance when her
supporters wished to punish the culprit who seized the
bangles. (37) The shawl and bangles were gifts from devotees,
and meant little to her. She was customarily benign towards
the socially depressed.

The full flavour of this situation only becomes evident
when it is realised that the Hindu-Muslim religious divide
was in process of negotiation. The thieves were low-class
Hindus, but Babajan declined to victimise them. There were
also beggars who typically pleaded for alms; these Hindu
people were often homeless, and could be pathetic in their
plight. Babajan would give them money that was gifted to her
by devotees. She would never keep any money for herself,
but always passed on the cash. She was also in the habit of
gifting visitor *faqirs* with incoming monies.

The *sepoys* were outnumbered by a swelling contingent
of local civilian devotees, comprising hundreds by 1920.
Some other middle class devotees travelled from Bombay
and towns like Nasik. A minority were affluent businessmen,
and in the 1920s they owned motor cars, the new status
symbols. Gatherings at the *neem* tree could be large, and at
times interrupted the cantonment traffic.

The devotee visitors comprised a Muslim majority.
Hindus were also represented, and likewise a minority of
Zoroastrians. (38) Babajan did not distinguish between people
on the basis of religion; she was indifferent to doctrinal
rigidities, and called everyone "child" (*bacha*). She did not
discourse or give sermons, but generally talked only very
briefly. She spoke in Pashtu, Persian, and Urdu (a dialect
of the Indian Muslims). She preferred allusive speech to
anything that might sound dogmatic. She did not promote

herself as a teacher. Her impact was in directions contrasting with the didactic approach.

Concerning her early days at Poona, Ghani relays: "Although shabbily dressed, there was something very magnetic in her personality, very unusual in the street mendicant that she looked, so that no passer-by could resist giving her a second glance." (39)

At the *neem* tree in Char Bavadi, Babajan sat on the ground in all weathers. Winter nights could be very cold; she would only wear a shawl as extra protection over her gown and trousers. She would often walk about in the cantonment and city streets. She slept very little, and her meals were small and irregular. She scornfully described the act of eating as *jodna* or "patchwork," meaning that eating was like patching a torn garment. The purpose was only to preserve the body, not to indulge it as the rich people did. Her jovial attendant (*mujawar*), in the 1920s, would accordingly use the same depreciatory word when bringing food to her. She was more partial to frequent servings of strong Indian tea, which visitors would offer her. She was known to give away her own food to hungry visitors.

> "She retained full powers of sight and hearing, and by all accounts could still walk as quickly as a girl. Her voice was nothing of a feeble quaver, but instead possessed an unusual depth and resonance that seemed to justify her masculine attribution. Yet the feminine characteristics of charm were in evidence.... Many have testified that the love emanating from Babajan was so intense that visitors felt pained at leaving her presence, departure involving the sensation of a powerful healing current being suddenly switched off." (40)

However, her varying moods included outbursts of anger, aimed at wrong approaches and bad habits. She was by

no means continually welcoming; sometimes she wished to
be alone, or with only a few persons. A full picture of Babajan
can only be gleaned from reviewing the diverse reports of
encounters.

In relation to the poor, she was exemplary. She
maintained a habit of sharing her simple meals with needy
persons. Devotees would frequently gift her with clothing
and other items (even solid gold bangles), but she was
basically indifferent to these. After wearing them for a while,
she would give them away to the poor. She would frequently
give away her shawl to someone with little clothing. Because
of such traits, local thieves would feel encouraged to steal
from her, feeling certain that she would not protest. A well-
known episode is that of the thief who tried to take a recently
gifted costly shawl from her. She was apparently asleep at
the time, and part of the shawl was pinned beneath her body.
"Her response was to raise herself a little without opening
her eyes, to help him [the thief] achieve his purpose." (41)

14. An Exceptional *Faqir*

A recent and brief academic version of Hazrat Babajan misinterpreted some events, causing confusion and indignation. This drawback missed out certain details on published record, evidencing a marked contraction of data and an unfavourable interpretation. Various related publications were entirely ignored. This superficial approach indicates the reductionism that can too easily occur, and which diligent scholarship is supposed to negotiate at all costs. The fact that this misleading treatment was published by a university press tends to underline the problem at issue.

I will here quote from one of the books omitted by the selective agenda. In an earlier work, I stated the following:

"It is still an unwelcome observation to some religionists and social scientists that exceptional 'underdog' individuals are more advanced evolutionary specimens than the status quo of the surrounding socioculture(s). I might here beg to cite the example of the Pathan matriarch Hazrat Babajan, a Muslim-born aristocrat who lived most of her life as a commoner and whose outdoor lifestyle was probably as archaic in its simplicity as can be found anywhere in the twentieth century. She lived in Indian environments dominated by the British, who found her an obstruction to military traffic in Poona....

"Feminists very often, and sometimes justifiably, accuse male writers of bias in ignoring female topics. I have, of course, met with accusation from male critics that *A Sufi Matriarch* (1986) is too short, but the extant data did not permit an increase into novelistic dimensions.

"Babajan's lifestyle in Poona consisted of a hardy outdoor existence seated under a tree. Such bare rudiments could, in an anthropological perspective, take her back many thousands of years to very archaic milieux. She is not for that reason to be considered even slightly primitive. Her cultural repertory was very complex, and not merely in its multi-linguistic cryptic expression. Some take the view that her lifestyle, though apparently primitive to modern tastes, was more compelling than the generality of modern lifestyles owing to the unusual psychological perspective in accompaniment.

"One may argue that it is more truly cultural to upgrade a squalid environment, as Babajan did, than to live amidst affluence and luxury and to degenerate via the proclivities of mass media, as too many moderns do. One hopes that there will be enough trees left to live under once the squalor of industrial sociocultures has bequeathed to the survivors an ecological desert that could have been paradise if inhabited by wiser nations or intercultural communities." (42)

15. *Wahdat al-Wujud*

*H*azrat Babajan is known to have made utterances implying her identity with the divine. These were not public proclamations, but spontaneous expressions arising from an introverted state. Such utterances had caused orthodox hostility at the time of her burial alive in North India, and later occurred during her early years in Poona. The utterances were sporadic and irregular, and quite unpredictable.

At Poona, orthodox Muslims are reported to have frowned upon these ecstatic utterances, which apparently gained exposure via hearsay. In contrast, her followers accepted these utterances in a context strongly associated with Sufi saints over the centuries. No close record of her statements survived, only a summary.

> "She was heard to say that she was God, that she was the source of everything, and that everything was created by her. Babajan was sometimes attacked for making such statements" (Purdom 1937, p. 20).

The "pantheistic" aspect of Sufism has an intellectual formulation in the teaching of *wahdat al-wujud* (unity of being), which has also been dubbed existential monism. This teaching is inseparable from the name of Ibn al-Arabi (d. 1240), and gained a strong profile in the annals of Indian Sufism, despite different interpretations. Many Indian Sufis believed in the validity of that gnostic perspective, although usually careful to accommodate their views within the framework of an Islamic religious setting.

The context for Babajan does converge with wujudi teaching, but at the same time, she was nothing of a systematic expositor. She was completely unconcerned with promoting any doctrine. She is not known to have composed any writing.

16. Encounters: Sufi Saints

Circa 1900, Babajan had appeared in Bombay for the second time, staying at Chuna Bhatti. There she had occasionally visited two Sufi saints in the metropolis, namely Maulana Saheb (Muhammad Hussein) of Bandra and Baba Abdul Rahman of Dongri. She characteristically referred to these entities as "my children," and they reputedly became her disciples. (43) However, there was nothing even remotely formal about the unorthodox Sufism of Babajan, who remained aloof from all the conventional exercises and affiliations of the Sufi orders. She did not teach any doctrine.

These contacts tend to bring out the Sufi associations of her career, which followed an unfamiliar and independent pattern.

One theory is that the reason for her appearance in Bombay was the access facility afforded for the *hajj* or pilgrimage to Mecca (Green 2009, p. 128). Bombay was certainly the major Indian port for pilgrim ships to Jeddah in Arabia. Muslim pilgrims from all over India and Iran favoured this means of access to the Hejaz. However, the theory may represent a simplification of her objectives, which remain unknown.

After her pilgrimage to Mecca in 1903, she returned to Bombay, and then journeyed north to Ajmer in Rajputana. This was apparently in 1904. There she paid her respects at the famous tomb of the Chishti saint Khwaja Moinuddin Chishti (d. 1236), but in her case, there was no subscription to the Chishti order. Soon after, she returned to Bombay, and then moved to Poona, apparently in 1905.

Concerning the "Sufi orders," associated with dervishism, a pioneering scholar wrote in 1969 that "no modern study of the orders exists" (Trimingham 1971, p. v). In India, there were four major Sufi orders surviving in the nineteenth century, including the Chishtiyya. These orders exhibited organisational and ritual dimensions, and represented a popular denominational form of Sufism. This phenomenon contrasted with the marginalised independent versions of Sufi life, whose exponents generally became obscured by legend and miracle story.

17. Encounters: The *Faqir* from Nagpur and Tajuddin Baba

*B*abajan is said to have encountered Hazrat Tajuddin Baba (1861–1925), a well-known Sufi *faqir* of Nagpur. This meeting is in question, requiring confirmation. One legend asserts that Tajuddin advised her to go to Poona (Burman 2002, p. 237). Legends easily arise around such figures. If these two did meet, the circumstances are unknown.

Tajuddin was originally a soldier (*sepoy*) in the British army. He was born at the British military cantonment in Kamptee, his father having the rank of a *subedar* in the Madras Regiment.

Tajuddin Baba gained repute as an eccentric Sufi, and annoyed the British when he once walked naked across a tennis court in 1892. He was arrested by the cantonment magistrate and sentenced to a lunatic asylum at Nagpur. Many years later, he was rescued by a local aristocrat, in whose palace Tajuddin thereafter stayed. His career has many complexities, including an endeavour to escape the attention of devotees and petitioners desiring spiritual and mundane benefits. (44)

A *faqir* who visited Babajan in Poona had recently visited Tajuddin Baba at Nagpur. This was *circa* 1920. The visitor had been well received at the settlement of Tajuddin, and had formed a good impression of that saint as a consequence. When he arrived at the *neem* tree in Char Bavadi, this *faqir* was disappointed with the rudimentary facilities attending Babajan.

"He went so far as to express his disapproval of the total lack of amenities for visitors, comparing her situation unfavourably with the lavish arrangements made for guests like himself at the abode of Tajuddin Baba. The matriarch silenced his incongruous complaint with the retort: 'What can Tajuddin give? He gives what I give him.' " (45)

This reversal of assumed priorities had an enigmatic complexion. Cryptic reference was an art of Babajan, and she appears to have employed this strategy frequently. She is known to have remarked, "Taj [Tajuddin] is my *khalifa* [deputy]." This would normally mean, in Sufi language, that Tajuddin was the disciple of Babajan.

Tajuddin himself had found that many visitors were merely bothersome nuisances, preoccupied with their own pet agendas and desires, which he was supposed to fulfil as their presumed mentor. The recourse he took to avoid these complications was more dramatic and elaborate than the tactics of Babajan. She always spoke of him respectfully, and even endearingly as Taj. When he died in August 1925, Babajan commented, "My *faqir* Taj has passed away." This remark caused puzzlement amongst her audience, but the next day, newspapers conveyed the fact of Tajuddin's decease at distant Nagpur.

18. Encounters: The Pilgrim to Baghdad

$\mathcal{T}$he word *faqir* was in general usage to describe Muslim ascetics. Many of them probably did not possess the talents and perspective of Babajan and Tajuddin Baba.

A visiting *faqir* came a long distance from Ajmer, where he had recently visited the famous shrine of Khwaja Moinuddin Chishti. There he had prayed for the means to undertake a pilgrimage to Baghdad and the celebrated tomb of Abdul Qadir Jilani (d. 1166). (46) By some channel or other, he was advised to approach Babajan as a means of achieving his objective.

When he arrived in Poona, the pilgrim requested Babajan for funds to continue his overland journey. She would not respond on this matter. For two days he stayed with her at the *neem* tree, but the issue of pilgrimage remained closed. He did not alter his preoccupation with Baghdad, which he evidently viewed as the most desirable destination.

Early in the morning of the third day, Babajan suddenly said to the visitor: ""You want to go to Baghdad, is that not so? Very well, you will go to Baghdad. I will send you there very quickly. Go to the road, and when I order you to fly, you should begin to move through the air. Do you understand?"

The gullible *faqir* was familiar with miracle stories in which Sufi saints had transported people over long distances. He was delighted at the prospect of a speedy culmination to his anticipated journey. He accordingly stood by the roadside, expecting to rise in the air when Babajan gave the signal. She dramatically rasped the word "*Orh*" (Fly). Thinking to aid the process, the *faqir* made a little jump, but soon found himself with feet still very firmly planted on the ground. He looked dismayed and turned towards Babajan, who asked him to continue. He obeyed, hoping every minute to defy the force of gravity. After a while, when his tension was becoming acute, she asked him to desist, and then exclaimed:

> "My good man, you wish to fly to Baghdad without wings, without money? Whoever suggested to you this trick? Do you sincerely desire to go to Baghdad?"

The forlorn *faqir* replied in the affirmative. Babajan then called into thin air: "Is there anyone around? Yes, well brother, see that this man reaches Baghdad." Ghani reports that she was in a "playful mood."

Within ten minutes, a wealthy devotee from Gujarat arrived, presenting Babajan with a purse containing three hundred rupees. She said immediately, "This belongs to Baghdadwala" (*wala* means man). She then threw the entire purse to the waiting *faqir*, and asked him to depart. He expressed his gratitude, leaving for Baghdad. (47)

It is evident that Babajan possessed a sense of humour. She was familiar with the mentality of tomb worship and *faqir* susceptibilities in miracle lore. Her visitor was intent upon the *baraka* (blessing) and spiritual benefits that he believed to reside in the famous tomb at Baghdad. The *neem* tree at Poona seemed trivial by comparison, not being on the same map of antique associations.

19. Encounters: Sheriar Mundegar Irani

A visitor with a different ascetic background was Sheriar Mundegar Irani (1853–1932), a Zoroastrian "ex-dervish" who had formerly travelled widely throughout Iran and India. His assessment of Babajan was radically different to that of the tourist ascetics who passed through Poona on their way to famed tomb sites associated with dervish orders.

To start with, Sheriar was a resident in Poona, and actually lived only a few streets away from Babajan's *neem* tree. The precise date of his first encounter with her escaped record, but may be attributed to *circa* 1910. He knew that the matriarch was very unusual, and understood her lifestyle better than most other observers. Nearly forty years before, Sheriar had reprojected his ascetic life on a journey from Bombay to Karachi, renouncing all the prospects of wealth that contemporary Parsis esteemed. He himself was an Irani, not a Parsi, and originally commenced his mendicant life in Iran, moving out from his native and oppressed locale at Yazd.

Ironically, Sheriar Irani's contact with Babajan was totally neglected in the official annals of the Meher Baba movement, eclipsed by the role of his famous son Merwan. That contact was preserved in oral channels, and also in a written format ignored by the Western sector of the Meher Baba movement.

Sheriar Mundegar Irani was a reticent man, not given to advertising his thoughts and discoveries, and confining his communications to relatives and close friends. He did not speak English. He was accordingly more difficult to locate in the published output of writers subscribing to the Meher Baba movement. (48)

This man appears to have been one of the earliest Zoroastrian contacts of Babajan at Poona. Sheriar Irani was not a devotee, but in a category more difficult to define. The varied Zoroastrian acquaintances of Babajan attest to the absence of religious bias on her part.

Sheriar was very familiar with events at Char Bavadi, and grasped the extent to which Babajan demonstrated a liberal inter-religious attitude. In Iran, his father Mundegar had professed allegiance to a (Shia) Muslim saint. In Poona, Sheriar tried to be of assistance to Babajan when possible. Like her, he was very sensitive to the fate of many Hindu poor in the city. The British generally tried to ignore the beggars and slums, as did the Hindu priests. Sheriar was grateful that Poona was an orderly place free of religious persecution. Nevertheless, the city was very prone to an insidious European mood of insularity against natives.

The Irani ex-dervish knew well enough about Parsi detractors of Babajan, and was averse to their narrow horizons. Some of these critics were conventional religionists who resented Muslims on the basis of Zoroastrian sufferings in Iran. Others were "progressive" secularists who detested anything ascetic, thereby distinguishing themselves from both Islam and Hinduism.

20. Encounters: Merwan Irani (Meher Baba)

$\mathcal{T}$ he most famous disciple of Babajan was Zoroastrian-born Meher Baba (1894–1969). His name of birth was Merwan Sheriar Irani. Born and reared in Poona, he attended the Deccan College, studying English literature. His academic life came to an end as a consequence of his contact with Babajan, in an episode that has frequently received comment, sometimes dismissive, though seldom with due analysis. The British occultist Paul Brunton misrepresented some details in the hostile version contained in his book *A Search in Secret India* (1934). The following quote comes from a non-devotee work which countered Brunton:

> "This matriarch [Hazrat Babajan] lived in the same cantonment zone of Poona as Merwan's family. It was in May 1913 that Merwan began to frequent her makeshift abode under the neem tree in the Char Bavadi locality. He visited her every evening, but their meetings were almost completely silent.... In January 1914 Merwan's mother Shirin was horrified to discover early one morning that he could not speak and was lying on his bed with wide open but vacuously staring eyes. He lay like this for three days to her even greater alarm.... Medical treatment produced no change in Merwan's extraordinary condition." (49)

Babajan definitely did exert a strong impact upon Merwan Irani. One day in May 1913, he rode past her tree on his bicycle. He knew that she was regarded as a saint by Muslims (and his father was fascinated by her). She was often guarded by tough Pathan *sepoys* from the nearby barracks, and most Zoroastrians feared to go near her. But that day, something happened to rivet his attention. She gestured towards him in welcome, and he dismounted from his bike.

Babajan then embraced Merwan, evidently with some fervour, and with tears streaming down her cheeks. She kept repeating *"mera piarra beta"* (my beloved son). He later said that he felt some kind of electrical current then passed through his body. He was so dazed that when he departed, he walked home, abandoning his bike.

Merwan subsequently lost interest in his studies and sports at college. Every evening he would visit Babajan at the *neem* tree, impervious to the soldiers. He would stay there for hours, sometimes until very late, hungry for the presence of Babajan, sitting by her side whenever he could. No words needed to be said. He was sensitised to an emanation, something which he could not communicate.

Merwan also encountered a problem. He found that Babajan was viewed by orthodox Zoroastrians as a kind of witch attended by fierce Muslim soldiers and afflicted by Hindu beggars. To such conservatives, a Muslim Sufi was an impossible guide. Orthodox Muslims viewed Zoroastrians in much the same way. Merwan himself became the target of Zoroastrian slanders in his new role as a disciple of Babajan. (50)

One night in January 1914, as he was about to leave the *neem* tree, Babajan kissed him on the forehead, and turning to the assembly nearby, she pointed at Merwan and said: "This child of mine will after some years create a great sensation in the world and do immense good to humanity." (51)

What happened next belongs in a biography of Meher Baba rather than Babajan. "He seemed to have effectively died whilst still physically alive." (52) It is relevant to narrate that Merwan's mother Shirin was so distraught at her son's acutely unusual condition that she complained to Babajan. The matriarch indicated that all would be well, although employing cryptic expressions. Merwan did gradually normalise, and in 1922 commenced an independent career as Meher Baba.

One of his later testimonies about Babajan reads: "Although wrinkled with age, she remained very energetic to the last, always looking bright, and usually cheerful. She had almost no wants, and there was no question of money in her life, which was that of a real *faqir*" (Stevens 1957, p. 64).

Some of Meher Baba's early followers had close links with Babajan. For instance, during the 1920s, a frequent weekly visitor was Savak Kotwal. Living in Bombay, this young Parsi (then in his twenties) would arrive at Poona by railway train on Sunday mornings. He would stay all day at Babajan's tree. On some of these occasions, Babajan expressed a desire to visit the Bund Gardens, an attractive place where she liked to sit for a short while. Kotwal would give five rupees for a *tonga*, meaning a carriage drawn by a horse or pony. Kotwal would follow in another *tonga*. He had "many unusual encounters with Babajan" (Kotwal 2006, p. 10). Kotwal subsequently became a devotee of Meher Baba in 1928 (Kalchuri 1988, p. 1051).

Another 1920s visitor to Babajan was Ardeshir S. Baria, a Parsi who became known as Kaka in his subsequent affiliation with Meher Baba. An engineer and motor mechanic, Baria lived in Bombay and owned several taxicabs. It is reported that he would never say a word to Babajan, despite his regular visits. One day she asked why he never made any request, unlike other visitors. He replied: "You are the Ocean and I am but a traveller who has come to drink from the Ocean" (Kalchuri 1988, p. 1067).

A regular visitor to Babajan at an earlier date was Sayyed Saheb Pirzade, a Muslim who was introduced to Merwan

Irani in 1918 by Babajan herself. This commenced a strong
liaison between the two. In 1920, Sayyed Saheb conferred
the name of Meher Baba ("compassionate father") upon
Merwan Irani, whom he revered (Kalchuri 1986, pp. 250,
290). Significantly perhaps, this name derived from the
Muslim sector.

21. Encounters: Sepoys

*D*uring her early years in Char Bavadi, regular visitors to Babajan at the *neem* tree included Pathan soldiers (*sepoys*). The Pathan warriors, now recruits in the British (or Indian) army, were famed throughout India for their fighting qualities and sense of dignity. Hindus, Muslims, and British alike were careful not to offend them.

Pathans were renowned for their physical strength. They were often tall by Indian standards. The soldiers wore turbans, and some were bearded. The British Raj liked to cultivate Pathan regiments after the 1897 revolt on the north-west frontier; the Pathan tribes had gained a reputation for fierce retaliation. Pathans easily adapted to the discipline of army life, and were regarded as a colonial asset.

Walking from the cantonment barracks, Pathan *sepoys* had a rendezvous at the *neem* tree in Char Bavadi, regarding Babajan as their own saint. These soldiers were distinctive, and a group of them could deter any loiterers and thieves. They formed what was effectively a private bodyguard in their off-duty hours. Their cordon was frustrated by Babajan's habitual sympathy towards beggars.

From 1914, Baluchi *sepoys* also made their appearance, being the medium for relaying the "burial alive" episode. "The heretic who had been buried alive now had her own corps of twentieth century janissaries." (53) A sceptical interpretation has suggested that the *sepoys* were eager to see miracles in the career of a *faqir*. However, the Baluchi testimony to a premature burial cannot be dismissed (see Chapter 8). These *sepoys* had formerly been in strong resistance to the matriarch.

The varying moods of Babajan included a fiery response. When roused, she had the typical Pathan hot temper, sometimes to a degree rather unusual in such an elderly woman. She was liable to pick up a stick (that she kept by her side) and adopt a threatening attitude. This gesture may be interpreted as a form of defence, and might have originated in the early days at Poona when Muslim children threw stones at her, encouraged by orthodox parents who regarded her as a heretic. (54)

The fiery mood of retaliation was also evoked by discrepant attitudes or habits in those around her. Some of the soldiers doubtless had rough edges; they could be surly toward non-Muslims. Whatever the cause involved, the *sepoys* would run away when Babajan got angry with them in these volatile situations.

> "When in a mood of *jalal* she would rise from the ground with flashing eyes and her stick in hand, the *sepoys* would run from the spot; even the strongest men in this group would not stay their ground. And so it was that these redoubtable warriors of Islam, who never flinched in the face of sword, gun, or cannon, nor shrank from sheer weight of enemy numbers, turned tail and fled from an old woman with a stick." (55)

Unlike the British, the Pathan soldiers were not alcohol consumers in their recreation hours. Like Babajan, they preferred to drink tea. Some Pathans in general are said to have favoured *ganja*-smoking, an activity that may have comprised a widespread barracks pastime in India. This factor is taken to an extreme in a very misleading interpretation, in which the Pathan soldiers at Poona are mistakenly represented as casual visitors to the *neem* tree, desiring to drink tea or smoke cannabis. (56) In reality, those

Pathans were genuine devotees, not Californian hippies (whose mindset disastrously influenced international trends from the 1960s onwards).

The *sepoys* wished to be in the presence of Babajan, whom they regarded as a saint and spiritual guide. They also wanted to protect her from interruptions, whether from local loiterers or hostile religious parties. In only a few years, the soldiers succeeded in cordoning the area against the local drunkards, drug addicts, and pickpockets, thereby strongly contributing to the transformation of Char Bavadi.

There is no evidence that the *sepoys* smoked *ganja* at the neem tree. Furthermore, this pastime seems to have varied greatly between Indian regiments, which could each comprise a number of different ethnic components. Even when it was favoured, *ganja*-smoking tended to be kept a secret, not being on view in public, especially where disapproving Christian missionaries could be encountered. Some British military officers liked to hear that "no man in the regiment smokes *ganja* or *charas*," which is one of the assertions found in early reports. There have been different opinions about the frequency of drug use amongst Indian soldiers during Babajan's lifetime. *Ganja* was usually smoked in a long clay pipe (*chillum*), and generally admixed with tobacco.

With regard to cannabis or hemp, there were three types of drug used in India, namely *ganja, bhang,* and *charas*. *Ganja* was widely smoked by labourers and other social contingents, and became a subject of debate during the 1880s, being opposed by some British officials and Christian missionaries, who also argued against opium. The Indian Hemp Drugs Commission of 1893–4 contributed a detailed survey. In 1925, cannabis was bracketed with opium in a new international regulatory system. See further Mills, *Cannabis Britannica* (2003). *Ganja* was still permitted in some regions of India during the 1940s, although subject to increasing strictures. *Bhang* was a beverage, prepared from cannabis leaves, an intoxicating drink to which Pathans were generally averse on religious grounds.

Charas was cannabis resin, being more addictive than *ganja,* and more notorious accordingly. Usage of *charas* was curtailed in India. See further "The Surprising Extinction of the *Charas* Traffic" (United Nations Office on Drugs and Crime – *Bulletin on Narcotics,* 1953, Issue 1, online article).

22. Encounters: Gustad N. Hansotia

A Parsi Zoroastrian named Gustad Hansotia (1890–1958) appeared on the scene in 1919. Born in Gujarat, he was reared in Bombay. For several years he had been a devotee of the Sufi *faqir* Sai Baba of Shirdi, visiting the latter frequently. Gustad had opted for a life of renunciation, and in this context, he became a disciple of Upasni Maharaj (d. 1941) after the death of Shirdi Sai in 1918.

Events were fast-moving. In December 1918, Upasni sent Gustad to Poona to assist Merwan Irani, soon to become known as Meher Baba. Upasni told Gustad to obey Merwan in all respects. Gustad had been fasting and looked very thin. He worked during the day at a toddy shop, following Merwan's instruction. The routine did not fit standard ideas of renunciation, and after a time Gustad began eating regular meals. Unlike Upasni, Merwan had no ashram, and his circumstances then lacked all amenities for accommodation.

Gustad was now instructed by Merwan to become the nocturnal attendant of Babajan at Char Bavadi. He was enjoined by Merwan to attend to every need and request of the matriarch. The *sepoys* were not present during the nocturnal hours, being part of the increasingly varied daylight occurrences. There may also have been a daytime attendant (*mujawar*) at this period. The role of attendant became a regular fixture at the *neem* tree, both day and night, serving to protect Babajan from unwarranted intrusions and to accomplish any necessary chores.

Gustad found to his surprise that Babajan did not sleep. As a consequence, he himself could not sleep when he wanted to do so. Winter nights in Poona were very cold, because of the high altitude, and he decided that Babajan should have a fire, himself feeling the need of one. This meant that Gustad would store wood at the toddy shop and carry this daily to Babajan's tree. He would carry the load on his head like a coolie.

The matriarch allowed this fire to remain. There was no ritual association, unlike the situation often found amongst other ascetics who maintained a sacred fire (often called a *dhuni* by Hindus). In her case, the fire was of purely practical significance.

The Parsi attendant marvelled at the effortless ascetic characteristics of Babajan. For instance, she customarily sat on the ground by the edge of the dirt road. There was never any seat or chair. After several months of his new vocation, Gustad suggested to Merwan that the matriarch should have something else to sit on instead of the cold hard ground. He apparently hoped that Babajan might rest more if she could lie down properly. A wooden platform or bed was then discussed. Merwan was in agreement, but insisted that Babajan would have to be approached on this matter first. She was not always amenable to suggestions. In this instance, she only agreed after some reluctance. Merwan then arranged to have the new furnishing constructed, and provided the money himself.

Some months passed. Gustad then suggested that a mattress should be installed on the wooden bed. Merwan guardedly told him to ascertain whether Babajan would agree to this further luxury. Gustad complied, but perhaps tended to press the matter. Babajan agreed, and Merwan again paid for the new acquisition. Yet this time, Gustad encountered a drawback. Babajan now said that he would have to carry the mattress wherever she went. It is a fact that she did not remain completely stationary at the tree, but would often move about the streets.

The very first night that the mattress was acquired, a downpour occurred. Babajan told Gustad to carry the mattress on his head, and he obediently did so, with the consequence that the new possession got wet. That night Babajan walked through the streets of Poona with some vigour, despite the rain, and evidently quite indifferent to the mattress being soaked. Gustad followed behind, the mattress absorbing more and more water in the incessant rain, and becoming heavier. Gustad now wished that he had not suggested the laborious addition. Afterwards, to his relief, the mattress rotted and became unusable. Babajan herself was not concerned with the comfort factor. Yet she did retain the wooden bed.

In these ways, Gustad was introduced to the temperament of Babajan. She was a rigorous world-renouncer, and not understood by some of her admirers. Babajan could be difficult and unyielding in the face of entreaties. Devotees could not be sure that she would agree to their suggestions or requests, which she did not always consider relevant.

Babajan did not take on disciples. There was nothing resembling the initiations and "teaching master" persona celebrated in the Sufi orders. Those who got close to her did find that a form of instruction or guidance was in process, but this was not declared or explained. Babajan did not ask for people to gather near her, and sometimes she was not responsive, preferring to be alone. There was local talk of miracles she had performed, but she herself was indifferent to this factor. The miracle lore evolved as a substitute for comprehension of her lifestyle.

Her pre-Poona history remained largely obscure. Only fragmentary reminiscences had ever been forthcoming, and then very rarely. Sceptics might attribute this to senility, but the indications are that she was simply not a self-promoter.

Merwan Irani appears to have ascertained her birthday as being January 28th (Purdom 1937, p. 109) but the year of her birth remained in oblivion. The birthday was commemorated at Meherabad during the 1920s. Yet the modern atmosphere of birthday celebrations, emphasising a pampered personal identity, was foreign to Babajan's own outlook. A factor she did emphasise was her "manhood," but this loaded gender topic was fleetingly uttered, and not dilated upon. Merwan would respectfully call her the "old man", a gesture which met with her approval.

Gustad believed that Babajan lived in a superconscious state, like Shirdi Sai Baba (and certain others), and that her actions could not successfully be measured by ordinary standards. However, he was not concerned to make such beliefs public in any way.

Later, Gustad became a full-time disciple of Meher Baba, although he still occasionally saw Babajan when he happened to be in Poona. He eventually observed silence at the instruction of Meher Baba, a discipline lasting until his death. This factor involved a curtailment of his reminiscences. Gustad is unusual for his varied encounters with no less than four of the mystical celebrities of his time. He became known as Gustadji in his later years, the suffix being a title of respect.

Details are supplied in my unpublished *Life of Meher Baba*. Some information is available in Kalchuri (1986, pp. 258ff.), who is surely correct in commenting that "Gustadji was a *fakir* [*faqir*] at heart."

23. Encounters: Mehera J. Irani

*A*nother type of contact is reflected in the account of Mehera J. Irani (1908–89), a Zoroastrian woman who became closely connected with Meher Baba. Her report describes events in 1924.

Mehera was living at Todiwalla Road in Poona with her sister Freni and mother Daulatmai. The latter's sister was Freny Masi, who is described as being close to Babajan. These women faced a problem with the local Zoroastrian community, who disapproved of the Muslim matriarch.

They would visit Babajan in the evenings, when many devotees attended after their daily work. Mehera says that her family group went in the evening for a different reason, the purpose being to avoid recognition from Zoroastrian critics, who would query "Why are they sitting with this old woman instead of going to the [Zoroastrian] fire temple?"

Daulatmai proved immune to the criticisms, and would also visit Babajan in the mornings, accompanied by Freny Masi. They would bring fruit and vegetables from the nearby shops.

Mehera relates that Babajan, because of her advancing age, now sat on a seat that had been made for her a few years before at the request of Meher Baba. Formerly she had sat on the ground in all weathers. This detail refers to the innovation associated with Gustad Hansotia in 1919.

In accordance with Indian custom, the male devotees sat on one side and the women on the other. "Babajan always sat so that she was turned more towards the men."

She habitually redistributed the food that was given to her, as she herself needed very little. She would also send someone to bring tea from one of the nearby stalls that had appeared. This commodity was shared likewise. Plaintive (and mystical) *qawwali* songs were often sung in Urdu (by a special performer, not by the audience).

"Babajan hardly spoke, and when she did it was very softly." Some of the men would talk to her, and she would "listen and nod her head, sometimes turning to see who was sitting amongst the women." Mehera refers to one occasion when Babajan turned to look at each of the women, and then a little longer at herself. "I was so surprised that she would look at me, and I felt very shy; Babajan hardly ever smiled, but now as she looked at me, she had a slight, very sweet smile on her face, as if she knew me." (57)

The impression conveyed is that Babajan was easygoing with women. She gave more attention to men, but could also express annoyance at obstructions and problems.

24. Encounters: Dhake Phalkar

*I*n 1925, Moreshwar Ramchandra Dhake Phalkar became a devotee of Meher Baba. This Hindu was originally a schoolteacher in Ahmednagar (he later gained a degree in law). Dhake, as he was generally known, was initially sceptical of non-Hindu mystics. His attitude has been described in terms of: "How can an Irani [Meher Baba] be a saint? What can an Irani teach a Hindu? No religion in the world can compare to Hinduism!" His mood changed when he moved to Meherabad and taught in the Hazrat Babajan School (Kalchuri 1987, p. 708).

In the late 1920s, Dhake and Rustom K. Irani were requested by Meher Baba to visit Babajan for two days at her *neem* tree in Poona. Many years later, Dhake supplied a description of events.

By now, Babajan had a fire burning in front of her. This detail is not found in other accounts (excepting that of Gustad Hansotia). Poona could be very cold on winter nights, and resorting to the comfort of a fire was then applicable.

"She was very fair in complexion but her body was shrivelled. Her face was all wrinkles running parallel to one another. She was toothless and had sharp eyes. Her voice was steady and loud enough to impress the audience. One of the fingers of her right hand was cut off. (58) She wore a silver ring on her third finger. She was always surrounded by disciples, most of them were Muhammadans. They would offer her tea often and she always enjoyed it. She did not allow anybody to bow down to her."

Dhake and Rustom encountered a setback when they tried to pay homage to Babajan by bowing down. She responded with angry words, emphasising the error. She even drove them away, requesting them to sit at a distance. Dhake indicates that such tactics were not unique to this occasion. "Sometimes she would chase them [visitors] away holding a brand in her hand." This reference apparently refers to a blazing stick taken from the fire. (The anti-homage attitude was not well assimilated in some accounts, including my own in *Sufi Matriarch*, p. 52; Babajan would allow Muslims to kiss her hand, but would not permit any obeisance or bowing down, this action being a strong tendency of Hindus.)

Rustom was a tall and sturdy Irani noted for his resourcefulness. In his new predicament, he ordered tea from one of the nearby stalls and offered this to Babajan. However, she insisted that the two visitors have tea first; only then would she take a drink herself. After a couple of hours, her fiery mood subsided. She then expressed pleasure that the two visitors had been sent by Merwan (Meher Baba), whom she called her son.

They spent two days and nights in her company, keeping wide awake (as they had apparently been instructed to do by Meher Baba). "Babajan was fluctuating in her moods, now calm, now angry." When they departed, she said in a mixture of Urdu and Gujarati, "*maro dikro, fateh ho gaya.*" Dhake supplied the interpretation that Meher Baba's work on this occasion was successful. (59)

25. Politics: A New Shelter and the British Raj

*A*n underlying factor concerning Babajan's life in Poona might be considered to have a political significance. "Not far away, almost within earshot, the army of the Raj performed their drill and the officers' wives assembled for decorous tea parties." (60)

The gulf between the British Raj and the Indian public was vast. The Poona cantonment, founded in 1818, was a training ground for troops. The "camp" was also an effective satellite of the Bombay administration and the Viceroy's distant mansion. The prestigious bureaucracy in London is also implied.

The early planning of the cantonment involved four square miles to accommodate European and native Indian troops. There were various amenities for the officers. Growth of the adjacent urban precincts was encouraged as a source of supplies for the army. The surrounding native populace were tolerated, but the British assumption of rulership was unassailable.

In her early years at Poona, Babajan resisted being dislodged from the *neem* tree in the face of British concerns about impeded traffic. The increasing number of her devotees was probably the clinching factor in her favour.

In 1919, after ten years or so at the *neem* tree in Char Bavadi, Babajan predicted that a destructive storm would hit Poona. This did in fact happen soon after. A tornado occurred, accompanied by heavy rainfall; trees were uprooted and some houses collapsed. Devotees pleaded with Babajan to take shelter in one of their homes, but she remained under the *neem* tree in accordance with her lifestyle of *faqiri*. She survived the severe weather, but the local devotees (reported to have numbered hundreds by this time in Poona) decided that a proper shelter must be provided for her instead of the makeshift awning of gunny cloth.

Hazrat Babajan quite literally lived on the level of India's poor. She had no assets, no possessions, and lived outdoors like so many of the street indigents. The comparison with colonial tendencies is pronounced.

The British Governor-Generals lived in a grand style, and annually retreated (along with other officials) to Simla for the purpose of escaping the summer heat. The British governing capital moved from Calcutta (now Kolkata) to Delhi in 1912. The construction of a Viceroy's House, or palace, was commenced that year, and was not finished until 1929. The final cost of this ambitious project soared to over £877,000, more than twice the figure originally allocated, and amounting to over £35 million in contemporary economic terms.

Permission from the aloof Cantonment Board was necessary for the comparatively trifling shelter which devotees desired for Babajan under the *neem* tree. The officials at first resisted, interpreting the gatherings of devotees (occurring by the roadside) as a serious blockage to traffic, including the new motor conveyances.

A few of the more prudent officials subsequently concluded that other problems could arise if public opinion was not catered for. The new political mood of the Non-cooperation movement had dented British complacency. Perhaps the Board began to worry about the Pathan and Baluchi bodyguards who had been in such evidence at the *neem* tree. These men were soldiers from the cantonment barracks, and the extent of allegiance was probably an X factor for military consideration.

The British army had advantageously assimilated strong native components, varying from the Nepalese Gurkhas to Baluchis, Pathans, Punjabis, Rajputs, and Sikhs. During the nineteenth century, the colonial army was formed in such a way as to comprise a ratio of "nearly one [European] to two [native Indians] for the army as a whole (65,000 to 140,000)." (61) This led to the situation where the British often relied upon native troops in emergencies.

A disaster occurred in April 1919 for the British interests. The massacre at Amritsar was hot news and much lamented. The episode was a British error and not a native one. The ultra-conservative Brigadier-General Reginald Dyer (1864–1927) ordered Gurkha and other native riflemen to shoot at the peaceful crowd in Jallianwalla Bagh at Amritsar. That action killed nearly 400 people and injured over a thousand. These are the figures given in official reports; however, other versions mention over a thousand dead.

"I thought I would be doing a jolly lot of good," Dyer said afterwards in justification. (62) Many British observers regarded him as a serious liability, the opposition including army officers and the British government. Dyer became known as the "Butcher of Amritsar." Twenty-five Baluchi and Pathan riflemen also participated in the massacre, and some officers may have feared what could happen if native troops ever fired the other way, as they did in the Mutiny over sixty years before.

The minority of Poona cantonment officials were successful in evoking a new Board decision to build at military expense a permanent weatherproof dwelling under the *neem* tree. The new Raj attitude now amounted to: "Hazrat Babajan had somehow become a celebrity, on their territory, and was their responsibility." (63)

Babajan's attitude to these developments was enigmatic. She allowed the workmen to build a structure of masonry and wood, with a roof of metal sheeting. This comprised a single room and a veranda. Prestigious members of the Cantonment Board then decorously invited her to move in to her new home. She flatly refused to do so.

The Board officials were now confronted with their error in having constructed the new abode a few feet away from Babajan's chosen position at the base of the tree. The tree was obviously very important (and far more so than the noisy and polluting motor vehicles now appearing, and which were so often deemed a municipal priority). Babajan is known to have exercised a sense of humour, evident from various episodes related about her. Now the Board (all males of course) had to devise a solution to their predicament.

> "An extension was made which connected the new dwelling with the trunk of the *neem* tree. The Board officials then gratefully retired from the scene, leaving Hazrat Babajan the virtual queen of Char Bavadi, legally installed in a British government building. As far as they were concerned, she had won." (64)

It is also reported that Babajan declined to occupy the new structure even after the extension had been made. She only consented to do so after strong pleading from devotees (Kalchuri 1986, p. 15). She was still complaining at the incongruity of a *faqir* taking comfortable shelter.

The new abode was open to the road on one side, but separated from the street by a low fence which guarded the veranda. Here Babajan lived for the last years of her life, in relative protection from the elements. She usually reclined upon her simple bed placed on the veranda.

26. Encounters: Dr. Abdul Ghani

Abdul Ghani (1894–1951) was not actually a devotee of Babajan, but a follower of Meher Baba. However, he did revere the former, and considered her to be exceptional. An Indian Muslim, Ghani had a strong empathy with Sufism, developing a close knowledge of the Perso-Arabic technical terminology. Ghani was more intellectual than many other devotees of Meher Baba and Babajan. He had a medical background in homeopathy, and had opened a dispensary in Bombay. Born in Poona, he had attended the Deccan College and Poona Medical School.

He shares an episode against himself. Ghani relates how, in 1922, when Meher Baba was staying in Poona, a few of the latter's early disciples from Bombay were allowed to visit him every weekend. The condition being that these men should first, before doing anything else, visit Babajan at the *neem* tree. Ghani (Dr. G.) failed in this respect, believing that he could conveniently see Babajan at night after attending to some other commitment. When he arrived late in Char Bavadi at about 10:30 p.m., he was informed by the attendants that Babajan was asleep. He saw that she was covered from head to toe with a white sheet.

Feeling rather deflated, Ghani sat close to the matriarch's bed, not sure what to do. He was startled when she suddenly threw off the sheet and physically attacked him. No harm was done, however. She also complained "You came [to Poona] in the morning and you come [to me] so late in the night!"

The visitor appears to have been shocked because Babajan actually knew of his laxity without being told.

This scene alarmed onlookers, but was over in seconds. Babajan then covered herself with the sheet, and seemed to go to sleep again. Ten minutes later, she got up once more and spoke to Ghani in a conciliatory vein. "My child, when did you come? Why did you not tell me when you had arrived? You must be feeling cold! Will someone get a cup of tea for this child?" (65)

In such situations, it would have been of little use to cite complex Sufi terminology. The action was instead one of surprise. The learned party here was really the learner.

27. Purported Miracles

*T*he careers of Sufi saints were often adorned with miraculous events by the writers of diverse compendia and hagiographies. In both Iran and India, this miracle lore became a convention. In the case of Babajan, Dr. Abdul Ghani added a supplement to his biography that became known as *Miracles of Babajan*.

Upon close inspection, the materials here are very diverse. Some of the content merely amounts to narration of unusual events, e.g. the episode of the *faqir* from Ajmer who desired to reach Baghdad. Ghani also included the episode of his own failure to arrive on time (recorded above). There is substantial factual detail in these reports.

Ghani was not a miracle-seeker, and believed that the greatest miracle Babajan had performed was the transformation of Merwan Irani (Meher Baba), whom he had known since childhood. Ghani did credit the matriarch with a 24-hour programme of "mental and physical healing." In a more general sense, he tended to concede the existence of miracles in the way that Indian Muslims often did, by way of association with saints. In this perspective, a "miracle" did not always mean anything fantastic, but merely amounted to an indicator of some prescience or ability.

A well-known episode relates to a theatre at Talegaon, a small town about twenty miles from Poona. One night a popular cast created an unusually large audience who filled the building to capacity. The management locked the doors in desperation, but afterwards fire broke out; a crisis ensued, with people struggling to get out of the building. At the same

time, at three a.m. in Poona, Babajan was seen to talk and
behave in an unusual manner, "quite excitedly and angrily."
Her words were reported by Ghani as: "It is fire, it is fire,
doors are locked and people are burning. Oh, you fire, get
extinguished!"

Persons who escaped from the burning theatre afterwards
testified that the obstructing doors "automatically opened"
(Kantak 1981, p. 48). Yet many people died in the blaze.
Devotees attributed the escape of survivors to Babajan's
intervention.

One of the miracle anecdotes concerns a blind Zoroastrian
boy, whose guardians took him to Babajan in the hope of a
cure. She "mumbled some words, and blew her breath upon
his eyes." The boy reputedly recovered his sight. Such a story
inevitably meets with scepticism.

Another tale was recounted by a motor vehicle driver,
who insisted that he saw Babajan near Shivapur, where he
offered her a lift. She refused, and he proceeded on to Poona,
where he saw her at the *neem* tree, there broadcasting his
discovery. "It could never have been possible for Babajan
to walk fourteen miles from Shivapur to Poona in half an
hour." Stories of saints being seen in two places are perhaps
fairly common in India, and do not convince sceptics that
any relevant event is in process.

Rather more interesting is the episode recounted by
Professor Hyder Ibrahim Sayani, a tutor of Persian and Arabic
at the Deccan College. In 1903 this academic travelled on the
same pilgrim steamship to Mecca as Babajan. He said that
she spoke in English to the European captain of the ship and
other Western passengers. This detail might be questioned,
were it not for a report in *The Times of India* dating to 1926;
the enthusiastic journalist (based in Bombay) here claimed
that Babajan spoke fluent English (Green 2009, p. 129).
Quite apart from this media report, Babajan does appear to
have possessed some linguistic dexterity in fusing different
language components (e.g. Urdu and Gujarati) in her speech.

Sayani apparently related that the pilgrim voyage to Mecca encountered a cyclonic wind, and the passengers lost hope of survival. Babajan is said to have told one acquaintance to beg a coin from every passenger and ask each of them to pray; they were enjoined to pledge (via prayer) that they would go to Medina and offer flowers at the tomb of Prophet Muhammad. The Europeans were included in this resort. As a consequence, all the passengers gave a coin and prayed in desperation. This is the kind of strategy that might have appealed to Babajan's sense of humour. However, the accuracy of the story is in question; pilgrimage hagiology was popular.

The 1903 *hajj* (pilgrimage) was first mentioned in 1926 by *The Times of India*. Although a miraculous element appeared in the narration, the basic event (i.e. the voyage) may be regarded as historical.

Another anecdote describes a visitor to Char Bavadi who wanted to take the matriarch to a nearby teashop. Babajan agreed, but stipulated that she would pay for the tea. The visitor was dismissive, saying "You are a *faqir*; where can you get money from?" At the same time he "very egoistically jingled coins in his pocket." Obviously, he was the man of the day where money was concerned. When the time came to pay, he found that he had lost the money in his pocket. His position did not look good. When they arrived back at the *neem* tree, he rediscovered his missing cash, which was somehow still in his pocket.

This is not really a miracle story, but an effective indication of a basic psychological drawback amongst some of Babajan's contacts. Affluence made them feel overconfident. They tended to assess events in terms of their own increasingly Westernised lifestyle.

28. *Faqiri* and Eccentricity

*T*he basic element of Babajan's situation was *faqiri*, the *faqir* lifestyle and outlook. The devotees and visitors were not uniform in their understanding of this factor. The Arabic word *faqir* is rarely comprehended today, and means rather more than "poor man", one of the translations in currency. An anglicised rendition is *fakir*, commonly associated with the stunt of lying on a bed of nails, a feat having nothing whatever to do with the psychological discipline implied in the vintage term. Snake-charming was another distraction.

Faqirs in India differed markedly in their attitudes and practices. They could be mendicant, stationary, superstitious, profound, eccentric, retiring, and at times assimilated to Hinduism. They were a minority in relation to the vast number of Hindu holy men. They often wore a traditional white robe (*kafni*), but some went naked like *sadhus*. Many *faqirs* were outside the Sufi orders, although some were loosely affiliated to one or other of these "dervish" organisations. There was no common rule, and the interpretation of "Sufism" could vary.

Some *faqirs* have been called *majzubs*. This identification bristles with difficulties of definition and context. Babajan herself has been called a *majzub* (Warren 1999, p. 200), but such ascriptions are generally loose. The term in question has been defined in terms of, e.g. "ecstatics who, ignoring all religious and social taboos, roamed about the streets of towns or in jungles" (Rizvi 1983, p. 470). This description does not entirely fit Babajan. Nor does the support phrase of: "Generally the *majzubs* ignored their visitors" (ibid.). The antinomian and extremist associations of the word *majzub* became a literary convention, leading to a stereotyped image.

Some of the *faqirs* resorted to drugs, like a number of Hindu holy men. These substances were not officially proscribed. There is no evidence that Babajan adopted this resort. She did not smoke *ganja* (cannabis) pipes, but was instead a tea drinker.

A confusion often occurred between *faqirs* and Hindu holy men. A well-known case appeared in the popular book of Paul Brunton, who supplied a photograph of Badreenath Sathu, an entity described by the identifying caption in terms of: "A faqueer (*sic*) who claims extraordinary occult powers. Here he is seen in a mystic trance wherein the eyeballs turn upon their axis" (Brunton 1934, plates). This man was not a *faqir*, but a Hindu *sadhu*. He is shown wearing a loincloth and adorned with body paint, wearing holy beads around his neck, and using a chin rest of familiar type. The pose is clearly ostentatious.

The confusion has also spilled over into other directions. Meher Baba has been described as "the Parsi *faqir*" (Green 2009, p. 186 note 148). A more appropriate description would be in terms of the Irani independent ascetic.

The British basically regarded Muslim *faqirs* and Hindu holy men as bizarre natives who could be tolerated providing they did not interrupt the process of colonialism. The situation was exacerbated when Mahatma Gandhi (1869–1948) became a symbol of Indian independence in the 1920s. His profile was depicted in terms of *Young India: Naked Faquir*, the title of a well-known book (Bernays 1932). The eccentric English renditions of a key word were almost endless (the original title of the Bernays book read *Naked Fakir*, and a related spelling was fakeer).

Gandhi was described as a "fakir" by no less an imperialist than Sir Winston Churchill, at a time when the Hindu leader encountered the British Viceroy, Lord Irwin, at the latter's resplendent palace in Delhi. The date was early 1931. Churchill was clearly in reaction to this meeting, and complained at:

> "the nauseating and humiliating spectacle of this one time Inner Temple lawyer, now seditious fakir, striding half-naked up the steps of the Viceroy's palace, there to negotiate and to parley on equal terms with the representative of the King-Emperor" (Fischer 1951, p. 348).

One may be certain that virtually nothing about "fakirs" was understood by the Empire elite. Babajan had far less chance of a hearing than a politician like Gandhi, who was clearly viewed as a fantastic upstart from the inferior native ranks.

By 1930, many Indians had become peacefully resistant in the Gandhian cause of *satyagraha*. The pronounced restraint of non-cooperation was violently met with the police baton (or steel-shod *lathi*). "The British beat the Indians with batons and rifle butts" (Fischer 1951, p. 345).

Babajan did not become part of any political movement. However, she did become a celebrity, surmounting the early difficulties caused by hostile religious attitudes (of conservative Muslims, and to a lesser extent, Zoroastrians). She did not criticise the British, unlike her male contemporary Bane Miyan of Aurangabad (who was the subject of an elaborate hagiography). Instead, the British too were her "children."

The basic *faqir* mode demonstrated by Babajan was the ideal of simplicity and abnegation, keeping no gifted money for herself, and abstaining from acquiring possessions.

Babajan did not seek fame. She sat under an obscure tree, and people were increasingly drawn to her. In addition to devotees, there were many visitors who wanted material benefits. She was averse to such petitions; in India, saints were frequently regarded as a medium for the gratification of desires for wealth and progeny. However, she was habitually kind to beggars by giving them money that she received from devotees. Many beggars were homeless.

The matriarch gained repute for being able to cure illnesses; however, she did not claim this ability. It would appear that she was sometimes exasperated by the people who persistently desired cures. Yet at other times she was sympathetic. Ghani describes her actions in the healing mode as "quite unique and entertaining."

Of the sufferer desiring a cure, she would say, "the child is being tormented by *goliyan*," the key word here meaning literally "small round pellets," interpreted elsewhere (by Meher Baba) as meaning impressions lodged in the mind.

> "To the amusement of those around, she would hold between her fingers the painful or diseased part of the person concerned, and calling upon some imaginary being, she would give two or three jerks to the affected part, simultaneously ordering the troublesome entity to quit. Surprisingly enough, this funny operation would impart instantaneous relief, and the party concerned would depart smiling." (66)

A contrasting instance occurred when a man suffering from fever begged Babajan for relief of his complaint. She then became angry, and took away the blanket he was wearing, telling him to pass that winter night in the open, in his exposed state. The next morning he is reported to have felt much better, his temperature having subsided. (67) This might be described as shock treatment.

Babajan is a relatively mild specimen of *faqir* eccentricity. The episode that critics have singled out is the "missing finger" phenomenon. Let me examine this here.

Her tolerance of ill-fitting metal rings might be considered a risk. She liked to wear rings on most of her fingers. The metals were brass, copper, and iron. One ring was too tight, and caused the finger to become infected and swollen. Babajan would not dispense with the ring, nor have the wound treated. A daily visitor from Nasik suggested an application of boric powder, but she reacted with annoyance. "Do you want to belittle my *faqiri*?"

She preferred to suffer pain instead of treatment. Eventually a Hindu devotee brought her a gift of mango pickles, a natural commodity which she tied directly upon the wound. The damage reputedly healed within a few days.

However, she did actually lose one of her fingers because of an ill-fitting ring. She would not permit the ring to be removed, and lost the septic finger instead. (68) This finger was infested with maggots. When these tiny creatures fell out of the wound, she would gently place them back on her finger and say "my children, feed and be at ease." Devotees wanted to take her to a doctor, but she refused. Nor would Babajan permit a doctor to visit her and treat the infection. The consequence was gangrene. "The finger wasted away and fell off." This damage healed, but devotees would shed tears at the sight. She dismissed their sentiment, saying that she enjoyed the suffering. (69)

A Western critic has referred to this episode in terms of a "ghoulish" manifestation of *faqir* tendencies. "As anyone who has met such a *faqir* knows, they have a certain ghoulish quality" (Green 2009, p. 132). A pronounced generalisation is evident here. *Faqirs* encountered by contemporary Western tourists are ghoulish, and therefore Babajan was too.

The association with *faqirs* at large can seem unreasonable. For instance, the wasting finger was not one of the popular *faqir* displays such as a bed of nails. Babajan's self-imposed trial was not a recognised exercise in mortification. She never engaged in exhibitionist stunts, for which some *faqirs* were well known. Her finger was lost because of the prized metal ring. However eccentric this episode may appear, the aspersion of "ghoulish" does not reflect her personality, and nor her interactions with devotees and visitors.

The indications are that Babajan was quite different to the general run of *faqirs,* especially those who cultivated stunts of ascetic prowess, frequently resembling routines of Hindu *yogis* and *sadhus.* Some of these exhibitionists claimed occult powers, which Babajan did not. Nor did she share other characteristics of the stunt men, e.g., to sit fixedly in a posture or pose supposedly proving transcendence. Her clothing was quite normal, featuring a white apron that resembled a *kafni,* along with white trousers that resembled secular attire. She did not wear the beads commonly associated with holiness, and nor earrings.

The self-inflicted lost finger is much easier to pardon than, for example, the fate of *satyagraha* pacifists who were "beaten and bitten in the fingers by [police] constables" after resisting confiscation of the salt they had made (Fischer 1951, p. 338). In 1930, the fraught situation caused by the British tax on native salt reached a new pitch in the baton attack by four hundred native policemen under the command of six grimly unrelenting British officers. The location was a salt works in Gujarat. Many hundreds of Gandhians were injured and some victims died. An eyewitness reported:

> "I heard the sickening whack of the clubs [batons] on unprotected skulls.... Those struck down fell sprawling, unconscious or writhing with fractured skulls or broken shoulders.... Hour after hour stretcher bearers carried back a stream of inert, bleeding bodies" (Fischer 1951, pp. 343–4).

While critics reject the stoicism of Babajan in the "lost finger" episode, there is a potentially significant detail involved. Even maggots were considered to have a relevant existence by the sufferer. This contrasted with both the orthodox Christian and Islamic attitudes to the lower species. Zoroastrians were in much the same category, their priesthood having preserved a custom of killing supposedly noxious creatures. In this respect, Babajan's elusive worldview clearly converged with *ahimsa* elements of Hinduism, Jainism, and Buddhism. *Ahimsa* means non-violence.

Babajan does not appear to have been a meat-eater. Her very sparse food basically consisted of vegetables and fruit, along with the frequent tea. Of course, the argument could be made that in Poona, she had lost her teeth, and so she would not have been able to chew meat.

Shortly before her death, she is reported to have visited the Sassoon Hospital, where she consented to a finger operation (Kalchuri 1986, p. 19). It is not clear what the problem was. However, the episode proves that she was not totally resistant to medical treatment at the very end of her life. The basic point to grasp is that she had been so remarkably robust throughout her years in Poona. *Faqiri* had done her no harm (save for one lost finger).

Babajan became well known for a resistance to medication and drugs. On occasions when she contracted fever, she would quickly recover without any medical assistance. The recovery time only slowed in the last few years of her life, when illness could be more severe.

29. Rocking to Sufi Music

*O*n many occasions at the *neem* tree, Babajan would permit *qawwali* music. She was not a puritan, and could respond strongly to this form of Sufi music. It is reported that, at such times of listening to *qawwali*, "her body would rock to the rhythm of its melody" (Kalchuri 1986, p. 15).

Devotees would enlist performers who were expert *qawwali* singers and musicians. This musical form is unfamiliar in the West, and accordingly requires some explanation. The Arabic word *qawwali* means recitation, and applies especially to the singing of Sufi poetry. There is a close relation to the Arabic word *sama*, meaning the act of listening to Sufi poetry, and which is the relevant term in medieval sources. The *qawwal* was the reciter or chanter, and in India was frequently an itinerant singer and musician (or a singer accompanied by musicians).

Sama was favoured by the Chishti order in medieval India, from the period of the Delhi Sultanate to the nineteenth century. The Chishti Sufis were opposed by the *ulama*; these religious scholars and legists sent complaining petitions to two Sultans of Delhi. The disapproving legists desired a royal decree to prohibit the musical sessions of *sama*. They were repulsed when the monarchs refused to outlaw the Chishti practices (Ernst 1992, p. 148).

A complex Chishti code was applied to *sama*, including rules of pure intention, and an encouragement "to seek genuine ecstasy (*wajd*) even if it meant imitating that ecstasy initially" (ibid., p. 149).

Acting outside the Chishti order, Babajan was quite independent in her patronage of *qawwali*. She did not advocate the imitation of ecstasy, but used her own *qawwali* events as a form of focus on spiritual themes. She was familiar with verses found in the extensive *qawwali* repertoire, existing in Persian and Urdu. She is reported to have frequently quoted such lines as:

"Despite millions of learned pundits and thousands of wise men, only God understands His own way of working" (Kalchuri 1986, p. 18).

30. Forthright and Cryptic Speech

$\mathcal{T}$he verbal expressions of Babajan were varied. She could give precise instructions detailing exactly what she intended, and make graphic comments to the same effect. There were also forms of cryptic allusion, combined with an admixture of languages. She could speak both Arabic and Persian, but often communicated in Urdu, a language more commonly understood by Indian Muslims. (70) Less fluently, she also employed Gujarati, a dialect strongly associated with the Parsi Zoroastrians of Western India. Her native Pashtu was more specialised in relation to Pathans.

In some abstracted moods, she would mutter constantly in an undertone. People who happened to overhear could not understand the meaning. She often seemed to be complaining or lamenting. There were times when she referred to atrocities inflicted upon her children. Speculations were aroused that she was bemoaning the loss of her children in the distant past. Yet Babajan referred to everyone as "child" (*bacha*). Relevant sources stress that she had no offspring. Another interpretation was that she empathised with harassed people who were not in her immediate environment. There were certainly vast numbers of people under pressure during the First World War and after.

One of her cryptic refrains was attended by a distinctive bodily gesture. She would say that vermin were constantly troubling her; however much she swept these pests away, still they gathered to bother her. Simultaneously, she would stroke the palms of her hands over her arms and body, as if removing cobwebs or insects, although no such problem was in evidence.

These allusions gained interpretations of a metaphysical nature, although Babajan herself did not supply any explanation. (71) Sceptics have rejected the interpretations, thinking that she must have been referring to mosquitoes or lice.

The cryptic allusions can be misleading, in that the matriarch was often very forthright in her speech. For instance, she was averse to being gifted with flowers, an offering which she considered impractical. She is reported to have scolded visitors with the refrain: "Why didn't you spend your money wisely on something like sweets or tea, which all can enjoy?" (Kalchuri 1986, p. 12). It is evident that Babajan viewed appropriate gifts in terms of something she could usefully redistribute to all those around her. She did not want anything superfluous.

The floral gifts were different to those generally favoured in Western countries. In India the bouquet generally took second place to a garland. Devotees hoped that the recipient would wear the garland around the neck. The action of garlanding could amount to the recipient accepting homage, and therefore Babajan was more averse to this procedure, as she resisted all gestures of obeisance.

The preferred sweets regularly featured in events. Ghani records that one visitor gifted Babajan with three *jelebis*, a type of popular confectionery. She gave these to a *faqir* in the audience. Another member of the audience complained at the favouritism. The sweets were considered desirable. Babajan smiled, and then called out: "Brother, bring sufficient *jelebis* so that each person here may get three." It was apparently not clear who was being addressed. Soon after, an "unknown man" arrived with a tray full of *jelebis*, the sweets being distributed amongst the crowd. Each person present is reported to have received three *jelebis* (Kantak 1981, pp. 53–4).

The various episodes concerning sweets, fruit, vegetables, tea, flowers, and *qawwali* music do not fit the description of "ghoulish", an adverse reflection aimed at the matriarch by a Western critic (Chapter 28 above). The interchanges included humour, profundity, and especially the redistribution of gifts.

Babajan was considerate of animals, and particularly liked horses. There were many horses visible on the Poona roads at that time, prior to the boom in motor vehicle technology. Indeed, a horse appears in one of the anecdotes concerning sweets. A man came to her who had lost his horse. Babajan pointed her finger in a certain direction, and told him "to go straight until the horse was found." The visitor quickly moved off as indicated, and soon found the horse coming towards him. The grateful owner then purchased a quantity of sweets, which he placed on the horse, taking these as a gift to Babajan. The visitor requested her to distribute the sweets with her own hands amongst the assembled gathering at the *neem* tree. Babajan complied, and also caressed the horse (ibid., p. 51).

Her asides to individuals could be brief but to the point. For instance, to a visitor who was experiencing a social predicament, Babajan said in Persian: "Always tell the truth, no matter how much it hurts you, or others" (Shepherd 1986, p. 55).

31. Last Years

$\mathcal{D}$uring the 1920s, Babajan became increasingly weak. Yet she retained full powers of sight and hearing, and could still walk easily. She would sit on her bed under the new shelter, visitors in front of her, but she would still walk about the streets when the mood took her.

By 1926, bigger crowds were assembling to see the matriarch. In September of that year, two favourable newspaper reports about her appeared in *The Times of India*. For many years, Babajan had been stationary at Char Bavadi, but now she agreed to be chauffeured in a motor car around the city. (72) She was escorted by Muslim devotees. This became a regular event. Her favoured halting place was the scenic Bund Gardens, where she liked to sit under a large mango tree overlooking the river Mulamutha.

> "For about two hours in the morning she would sit under this tree, giving audience in her accustomed manner of warm responses, flashing rebukes, cryptic allusions, and terse instructions. A prominent Muslim citizen made it his regular duty to send her breakfast, and this she would characteristically share with her pupils and visitors." (73)

The location was rather appropriate in an ethnic context. The Bund Gardens was a public access property created by the Parsi tycoon (and philanthropist) Sir Jamshetji Jejeebhoy (1783–1859). This influential merchant compensated for the fact that all natives were prohibited from entering other parks in Poona by the "European only" mentality of the Raj

(Green 2009, p. 131). In Poona, the whites were generally promoted as superior, and all Indians were secondary, scarcely recognisable in advanced society. The natives were of some use as soldiers and servants, but could not walk in elite precincts.

On April 1st, 1928, Babajan left Poona for the first time on a day excursion. For many years she had never gone outside Poona. Now she made an unexpected motor journey to Meherabad, the ashram of Meher Baba near Ahmednagar. Here, the Hazrat Babajan High School had been established, an independent project named in her honour. However, that school was not the purpose of her visit. During the past week, she had emphasised her wish to visit Meherabad, or more specifically, "the place of my child." She was discovered to be constantly referring with affection to Meher Baba. This development was in low profile, and resultant events were not anticipated at large.

After a journey of some three hours with Muslim escorts, Babajan alighted from the car at Lower Meherabad. The time was about 11:30 a.m. Meher Baba was on the hill (Upper Meherabad), across the railway tracks. On being informed that she had arrived, Meher Baba came down from the hill and stood about fifty yards away from her on the other side of the railway line. There was no actual meeting between these two mystics. He asked his *mandali* (resident devotees), and also others, to greet her one by one.

While this unusual event was in process, Babajan conducted a monologue which the *mandali* found difficult to comprehend. They grasped that she was praising Meher Baba, but she also "referred to many spiritual secrets which the *mandali* could not follow" (Kalchuri 1988, p. 1037). Distinctive cryptic speech was here witnessed.

The visitor consented to drink a little water, but wanted nothing else. Her purpose had clearly been served, and she departed shortly after. Meher Baba remained standing throughout on the other side of the railway line. After Babajan had departed by car, he remarked that "today is the most eventful and significant day of my life." He did not explain the reason.

The following day, he made a return visit to Babajan, again by car. The scene was the Bund Gardens, where Babajan sat with a group of Muslim devotees. Again there was no direct meeting between herself and Meher Baba. The visitor remained at a distance, standing on the opposite bank of the river, sending his *mandali* to greet her via a nearby bridge. (74)

These atypical "meetings" did not receive any publicity. There were no cameras, no interviews, no newspaper reports.

Babajan repeated her visit to Meherabad a few weeks later, on May 8th, 1928. This occurred when Meher Baba was driven by car to Poona that same day. So this was not an encounter between the two. When she arrived without warning at Meherabad, she had an audience with the devotees and Prem ashram boys who were present. She was noticed to be especially considerate of the boys, as they met her one by one. Again, there was no publicity attending the visit. On the return journey, Babajan's car passed the vehicle escorting Meher Baba on his way back from Poona. (75)

A further contact occurred on October 5th, 1928. The location was Ahmednagar, where Meher Baba was sitting on the veranda of a devotee's home. A car unexpectedly arrived, with Babajan a passenger. Her vehicle stopped close by, and there followed "an exchange of glances" between her and Meher Baba (Kalchuri 1988, p. 1101). Babajan's car moved off after only a few minutes. Meher Baba attached a cryptic importance to the episode.

32. Encounters: Paul Brunton

A British occultist recorded his meeting with Babajan during the last year of her life. Paul Brunton (1898–1981) included a carefully edited account of this event in a commercial book entitled *A Search in Secret India* (1934). The episode was part of a short stay in India. The book became a bestseller, but has been attended by strong retrospective criticism. Significant details were missing.

Brunton's account is undated throughout. However, the relevant dates have been researched. Brunton arrived in Poona in late November 1930, accompanied by his interpreter, who was none other than Jal S. Irani, a brother of Meher Baba. The identity of the interpreter is altogether missing from *A Search in Secret India*, which is just one of the discrepancies in evidence.

Brunton says he was warned by his interpreter that prolonged conversation with Babajan was not permitted, because of her weakened condition. He describes her lustrous white hair, heavily wrinkled face, and feeble voice. She was lying on her bed under the shelter at the *neem* tree. Her head was propped up by pillows.

Verbal interchange was at a minimum here. Brunton introduced himself, and the matriarch clasped his hand, "staring up at me with unworldly eyes." After a few minutes she withdrew her hand, and then said something to Brunton's intermediary. The language was not English, and so Brunton could not understand what was said. A translation was made. Only a short sentence was reproduced: "He has been called to India and soon he will understand."

Back at his hotel afterwards, Brunton found that contact with Babajan had produced an effect, altering his customary thinking patterns. "That some deep psychological attainment really resides in the depth of her being, I am certain." (76)

Brunton "included the meeting [with Babajan] in his subsequent book, but in a manner very favourable to his own talents, and the account may therefore be studiously incomplete." (77)

The Western writer also included a very brief and inadequate version of Babajan's life. He favoured the interpretation of a Parsi in Bombay named Khandalawalla, a former magistrate. Brunton had met this man briefly, and shortly before he moved on to Poona. Brunton says that Khandalawalla had known the matriarch for fifty years, which is extremely unlikely. One should be critical of the duration proposed. Thirty years perhaps, conceivably dating back to Babajan's sojourn in Bombay; there is no evidence of a close association, however. Brunton is the only source for this contact. Khandalawalla favoured the belief that Babajan was born in Baluchistan, but with no accompanying details.

Brunton's version attributes the new shelter at the *neem* tree to "some Muhammedans", oblivious to the complex series of events involving the Poona Cantonment Board. A mood of contraction was preferred by Khandalawalla, who was eager to curtail the high estimates of Babajan's age, maintaining that she was "really about ninety-five." (78) The truth is that nobody really knew how old she was; the date of birth had gone into total obscurity.

Khandalawalla conceded that Babajan was "a genuine faqueer (*sic*)." However, a basic antagonism towards Meher Baba is evident, and also the latter's Hindu teacher Upasni Maharaj, (79) to whom Khandalawalla attributed the financial catastrophe of his son-in-law on the Bombay Stock Exchange. Here we arrive at a basic psychological divide in these matters. Upasni Maharaj was an ascetic, and cared nothing for the values attaching to stock exchange shares, which ranked high in secular Parsi activities.

The agitating Khandalawalla was affiliated to a worsted contingent of (male) Parsi Zoroastrians who had for many years ridiculed Babajan as an ascetic alien, one remote from their own cultural value system. This opposition was in occurrence during the *circa* 1910–1920 period. The detractors were disconcerted when Babajan became well known as a Muslim saint and was legitimated by the Poona Cantonment Board. The critics were obliged to discreetly abandon their petty calumnies. Meher Baba became the new target of their animosity; this attack was sometimes of a religious nature, and sometimes of a secular complexion. The assailants spread vindictive rumours about Meher Baba that he was easily able to dismiss. Khandalawalla was relatively generous in the admission that the Irani was honest and really believed in his spiritual attainment.

Asceticism was a lifestyle completely different to preferences of Parsi conservatives and modernists; they frequently agitated against this rival. In contrast, Brunton's own approach to ascetic roles was influenced by an interest in occult powers. For example, he could write: "Is it possible that... this haggard and huddled figure [Babajan] contains the soul of a genuine faqueer (*sic*) with wondrous powers?" (80)

Brunton's mood of critique in relation to Meher Baba is unreliable in a number of particulars, including his notorious depiction of the Irani as having a deficient cranium. Retrospective assessment of Brunton was given an edge by one of his former admirers, Dr. Jeffrey Masson, who shatteringly revealed, for instance, the spurious nature of a doctoral (Ph.D) credential claimed by Brunton during the 1940s. (81)

33. Last Months and Death at Poona

*D*uring her final years, Babajan was prone to recurring attacks of fever, and could spend days in recuperation lying on her bed. As of old, she had the ability to recover completely, without resorting to medication.

Paul Brunton's confusing account gives the impression that she was bedridden and decrepit. In fact, she was still engaging in local car journeys on some days, and on one occasion travelled much further, indeed to Meherabad ashram near Ahmednagar, which she had visited in 1928.

Her purpose was to see Meher Baba. This clandestine meeting occurred in the summer of 1931, and was little known for many years. There were complex preliminaries, and eventually Babajan instructed a Muslim devotee to escort her by car to Meherabad. The destination was Meherabad Hill, where Meher Baba was in residence. In contrast to the situation in 1928, no colony was existent at Meherabad in 1931; only a few of the *mandali* were now living at this largely deserted ashram.

Babajan alighted from the car at the foot of the hill. Meher Baba emerged from his hut. For a long time, the two saints stood silently facing each other. Babajan was the only one of the two who spoke (the other had observed silence since 1925). She is reported to have called out loudly: "It is time for me to go, Merwan! Why don't you set me free?" (82)

This encounter was not advertised in any way. Only a few persons witnessed the event. Interpretations of the episode were in very low profile.

Meanwhile, Muslim devotees created a Trust for Babajan's prospective funeral and the construction of a shrine (*dargah*), assisted by a gift of 4,000 rupees from Meher Baba.

Although the Cantonment Board had endorsed the shelter under the *neem* tree, the new group of trustees anticipated that the military authorities would refuse permission for Babajan's burial within cantonment precincts. Accordingly, they investigated sites in other parts of the city, but were unable to reach a unanimous verdict as to which was best.

Eventually, they approached Babajan herself in order to resolve this matter. They were unprepared for their reception. She erupted into a rage over the issue. "Get away from here!" she exclaimed. "How can the dead show concern for the living? I am not going to leave this place." (83)

She thus made clear her wish to be buried at the *neem* tree, regardless of official red tape. The British military authorities were apparently implied as the deceased party (certainly, they had less than two decades left of supremacy in India). The trustees accordingly forced the issue with the Cantonment Board, and the proposal was agreed.

A few days before she died, Babajan was heard to mutter: "It is time for me to leave now – the work is over. I must close the shop." One of the devotees objected to this prospect, but she responded: "Nobody wants my goods; nobody can afford the price. I have transferred my goods to the proprietor" (Kalchuri 1986, p. 19).

Hazrat Babajan died at Poona on September 21st, 1931. "Her funeral procession was a tremendous affair, never accorded to any dignitary or royalty in the annals of Poona." (84) Thousands of Muslims and Hindus are reported to have attended the funeral. The female *faqir* had triumphed over all odds.

A marble tomb was built at the spot where she had lived under the *neem* tree, in accordance with her wishes. She did not leave behind any new doctrine that could be turned into a system.

34. The *Qalandar* Issue

*B*abajan did not promote herself as a teacher, and never appears to have made any claim about being a Sufi. She did not give any name to her role, other than that of *faqir*, meaning ascetic or renouncer. However, when she used the word *faqir* (as she did quite often, it seems), she meant the basic form of Sufi vocation, going back centuries before the dervish orders of the medieval era (and when more women were in evidence as scholars and ascetics).

In Sufi history, there were instances of the female *faqir* role, but for the most part obscure and unfavoured in the conventional reports subsequent to the era of early Sufism. "Some [dervish] orders admitted women as affiliated members, though relatively few had dervishes, *faqirat* [female faqirs] or *khawatat* [female dervishes]." (85) The independent role exceptions like Babajan fit a borderline category.

"Female mystics frequently became hermits or solitary dervishes, and frequently had to live without the comforts provided by the system of *pirs* (preceptors) and *khanaqahs*." (86) The Sufi *khanaqah* or hospice was a male-oriented institution, and spread from Iran into India during the medieval centuries.

Babajan did not assert the importance of *shariat* (religious law), in contrast to many orthodox Sufis. Yet neither did she militate against Islam in any way. She was liberal towards Hindus, but was averse to any act of homage in her direction; such obeisance was associated with Hindu *darshan* customs. She had undertaken the pilgrimage to Mecca more than once. It is not clear whether she performed the daily prayers.

There were different views about the prayer ritual (*salat*) in Sufi ranks. "When a Sufi was completely lost in ecstasy for a period of days, or even weeks, he was exempt from praying" (Schimmel 1975, p. 152).

Ghani urged a theory that Babajan represented the beginning of a "Qalandari era" in which "the characteristic feature will be the universal dissemination of spiritual truths and divine secrets, however unpalatable they may be to traditionally vested interests." (87)

Ghani refers to Babajan "as possessing all the characteristics of a Qalandar," a conclusion based upon his definition of *salik-majzub*. (88) This theme does not address the problems in Sufi history relevant to the *qalandar* phenomenon, complications that were little known in scholarship of the 1930s. It is obvious that Babajan's very unusual career posed Ghani with a dilemma of description for which no adequate terminology existed.

The *qalandar* equation is not satisfactory in view of the association with male itinerants of an earlier era who could tend to an antinomian orientation. Many had denied the relevance of formal religious observances, but some were extremists who opted for a libertine lifestyle. The ambiguity posed by this role is reflected in the modern statement concerning "*qalandars*, who resembled dropouts rather than ascetics, and who were known more for irreverence and bizarre behaviour than for their observance of religious proprieties" (Ernst 1992, p. 17). In contrast, Babajan was not irreverent, and definitely was an ascetic.

The *qalandars* varied greatly in their disposition, and included Shams al-Tabrizi, the inspirer of Jalaluddin Rumi (d. 1273). The wandering dervish Shams is thought to have been a *qalandar*, and did not fit well into the class society of Qonya, influenced by the theological elite. He disappeared from the scene in 1248. One traditional source (Aflaki) affirms that Shams was murdered. This was apparently at the instigation of Rumi's son, a religious professor of local status. (89) The situation seems a graphic reflection of the more extensive friction occurring between different lifestyles and psychological orientations. The complexity being that Rumi himself was a professor of religious learning, although one who now became a mystic.

Shams is thought to have been of artisan origin. (90) To what extent this detail may reflect the *qalandar* background as a whole is uncertain. It is, however, obvious that the majority of *qalandars* were not from the upper classes, including the *ulama*.

The *qalandars* were definitely a male phenomenon, arising from a mendicant impulse that contrasted with the settled and affluent milieu of "moderate" Sufism represented by the hospices or centres. The radical trend mushroomed during the thirteenth century in different countries, and took varying forms. A monastery of *qalandars* was founded near Cairo during the 1290s, by the Iranian ascetic Hasan al-Jawaliqi. In India, the homeless itinerant *qalandars* reacted to the settled "Sufi centre" lifestyle of the Suhrawardi and Chishti dervish orders. The Chishti annalists represented the critics as being sacrilegious, but also conceded that some of the radicals were genuine mystics. (91)

There were large numbers of enthusiasts and hangers-on, and in the absence of appropriate tuition, excesses and peculiarities occurred. In Sunni India, the qalandariyya became substantially assimilated to the milieux of Sufi (or dervish) orders, while in Shi'ite Iran the minority trend became notorious for nonconformist tendencies, including resort to opium and wine.

The thirteenth century conservative Sufi classic *Awarif al-Maarif* sceptically refers to the *qalandar* as seeking to destroy accepted custom. (92) There were two sides to this argument, as is clear from the sources. Seven centuries later, Babajan did not militate against accepted custom, and did not encourage devotees to be antinomian or reckless in any way. However, the aspersive description would fit some male *qalandars* in Iran and India.

Some *qalandars* converged with Hindu Yogis in resorting to hemp and other drugs. They also favoured the practice of wearing earrings, their pierced ears apparently copied from the Nath Yogis. *Qalandars* also included the extremist ascetic grouping known as the Haidariyyah, named after the Turkic saint Haidar who lived in Iran. His followers pierced their bodies with iron rods and rings as a form of penance. The disciples of a prominent Indian Haidari leader were responsible for mortally wounding the "political Sufi" known as Sidi Maula, a thirteenth century event. (93)

Subsequently, a well-known Chishti leader, Nasiruddin Chiragh (d. 1356) was stabbed by an aggressive *qalandar*. Yet numerous of these itinerants in India were absorbed peacefully into the Chishti and Suhrawardi orders during the medieval era. In the thirteenth century, many *qalandars* in India began to adopt the settled lifestyle revolving around the *khanaqah* or Sufi centre. Later, other *qalandars* attached themselves to the Nimatullahi order, based at Kirman in Iran, and which commenced in the fifteenth century. (94)

The activity of early Chishti Sufis occurred in association (and friction) with the Turkish aristocratic and military class that ruled India during the thirteenth and fourteenth centuries. These people, and the *ulama*, were the audience for Sufi works, which encouraged a belief in the power of saints as intercessors with Allah. There was a big gap between the elite (*ashraf*) classes and the commoners.

"Many leading Chishti disciples were members of the court or the administration" (Ernst 1992, p. 88). Hagiography depicts some Chishti saints as refusing to accept land endowments, to avoid dependence on the court. "They nonetheless relied on gifts from all classes of society, especially the wealthier classes" (ibid.). Indeed, Sufi circles even adopted court ceremonial at that time. There was evidently room for *qalandar* complaints.

Establishing factual events can be difficult in this field. "Some of the stories in *Siyar al-awliya* [Lives of the Saints] are not descriptions of actual events at all, but are narrative elaborations of Sufi maxims and popular stories" (Ernst 1992, p. 86). That text is considered one of the more reliable early Chishti sources, written *circa* 1350 by Mir Khwurd, who was nevertheless partial to miracle lore.

Certain other texts have gained the negative description of "unrestrained hagiographies," such as *States of the Chishti Shaykhs*. This late fourteenth century work adopts the format of a chain of succession (*silsila*), commencing with the Prophet Muhammad and thereafter featuring seventeen master-disciple transmissions ending with the author's own teacher. "Practically every anecdote in the book is a miracle story" (Ernst 1992, p. 87).

The same extravagant text relates how the Chishti founder, Moinuddin Chishti, while meditating at Mecca, "was granted the boon that all future disciples of his line would be blessed by God" (ibid., p. 88). This kind of reassurance for posterity recurred "not only in Sufi hagiographies but also in political chronicles that legitimise dynasties in the names of Sufi saints" (ibid). Obviously, there were many people who became interested in such guarantees, and perhaps not always for sublime reasons.

The Chishti *khanaqah* "consisted of a big hall called a *jama'at khana* in which the followers lived their communal life" (Lapidus 1988, p. 448). There is a democratic element discernible, although the Sufi leader was uncontested, and some of these men were associated with the prestige role of *qutub* celebrated in Sufi hierarchy lore. The Chishti leader "received the general public, listened to petitioners, gave amulets to heal the sick, mediated disputes, and dispensed spiritual counsel" (ibid.).

One of the earliest Chishtis was Baba Farid, known as Ganj-i Shakar (d. 1265), who refused to live in the capital of Delhi, and instead resided at Ajodhan (Pakpattan), a small town in the Punjab. In this manner, he steered clear of problems with the Turkish Sultanate. A competitor was Bahauddin Zakariya, the wealthy Suhrawardi *shaikh* of Multan. Baba Farid "contended with political intrigues from jealous local officials; he even survived assassination attempts" (Lawrence 1978, p. 23).

Spurious collections of discourses (*malfuzat*) were foisted upon the early Chishti saints by anonymous writers, who were actual contemporaries in some instances. These fabrications "catered to the insatiable popular taste for details of the miracles of mystics, as well as those of yogis and qalandars; they also provided for the proselytising militancy of many Muslims whose concerns were not really with Sufism, but in the assertion of their own superiority in the field of religion" (Rizvi 1983, p. 5).

The *qalandars* subscribed to the same monistic teaching (*wahdat al-wujud*) that was favoured by many "moderate" or "orthodox" Sufis, including Chishtis. This teaching, set into a form of theology, could vary in emphasis. The wujudi teaching originated (95) with the Andalusian Sufi Ibn al-Arabi (d. 1240). In contrast was the more conservative *wahdat al-shuhud* of the Iranian Sufi Ala ad-dawla as-Simnani (d. 1336). The shuhudi doctrine later recurred in the Naqshbandi order. (96)

The *qalandar* phenomenon continued into the Mughal era, with diverse permutations of role. The Chishti *shaikh* Abdul Quddus Gangohi (d. 1537) encountered Shaikh Husain of Jaunpur, who "had given up obligatory [religious] things altogether, although he was a profound scholar." (97) These two entities were very different. A bone of contention was here daily prayers. Fantastic explanations for such omissions were by then in vogue amongst supporters of *qalandars*.

Shaikh Husain "wore a rag that just covered his nakedness and he had no means of livelihood; still he possessed a big library; people came to see him, but his mind seemed to be elsewhere and he did not attend to anyone." (98) Later, in the seventeenth century, a well-known *qalandar* (and *majzub*) was Sarmad, an Islamised Jew from Iran who favoured going naked like Hindu ascetics; this outspoken radical clashed fatally with the influential *ulama*, being executed during the reign of Aurangzeb. (99)

In the nineteenth century, Richard F. Burton referred to bizarre *qalandar* customs occurring in Sind, which included branding on the shoulder with a red-hot iron. The drunkenness and debauchery of some contemporary *qalandars* contrasted with the celibate reputation of Lal Shahbaz Qalandar (d. 1274), whose famous tomb at Sehwan was a major pilgrimage site (Burton 1851, pp. 208, 211). Lal Shahbaz is a largely legendary figure, associated with tolerance of Hindus.

In some aspects of her career, Babajan did sequel the early *qalandar* itinerant spirit of independence from the *khanaqah* system spread by the Sufi orders. That system was associated with a doctrinally hidebound "orthodox Sufi" establishment. Babajan's early contact with a Hindu teacher is reminiscent of the medieval *qalandar* tendency to affinity with Hindu ascetics, which took varied guises. She was discernibly in affinity with the *wahdat al-wujud* teaching, as demonstrated by her gnostic reveries (or ecstasies) that were unwelcome to orthodox Muslims.

Professor Rizvi stressed that "the biographies of a large number of [Sufi] saintly women remain unknown.... Female sufis were generally hampered in a number of ways.... Female mystics were never incorporated into *khanaqahs* and orders as spiritual succession could not be traced through them. Often they became hermits or lone dervishes.... It would not be unfair to say that, Muslim women who became deeply committed to mysticism and a life of asceticism did so in spite of a lack of encouragement and assistance from their male counterparts and from Islam in general." (100)

As a consequence of these considerations, the neo-*qalandar* context for Babajan needs due appraisal in terms of a female (or professed "man") role that is virtually unknown in the traditional annals.

35. Women and Sufism

$\mathcal{T}$he life of Hazrat Babajan is relevant to the factor of women in Sufism over the centuries. Unfortunately, the record is very uneven, although dating back to an early period.

The British scholar Margaret Smith wrote that the development of Sufism (*tasawwuf*) within Islam gave women their opportunity to attain the rank of sainthood. Some male Sufis awarded to a woman the prominent role among the earliest Muslim mystics, choosing her as the representative of the first phase of mysticism in Islam. This was Rabia al-Adawiyya (died c. 801), an Arab freedwoman of the Al-Atik, a tribe of Qays ibn Adi, from whom her name derives. She is celebrated in tenth century Sufi sources, and several generations later, Fariduddin Attar urged in his *Tazkhirat al-Awliya* (*Memorial of the Saints*) that saintship (*wilaya*) may be found in a woman as naturally as in a man. Islam had no priesthood and no priestly caste, and so in theory at least, there was nothing to prevent a woman from reaching the highest religious rank in the hierarchy of Muslim saints. Yet despite the fact that writers of repute like Attar and Jami made many references to women Sufis, Muslim theologians and legists were liable to denounce women saints.

Rabia has been viewed as making the greatest contribution of any woman towards the development of Sufism. However, there were also other women of her time, and many more after her, who were regarded as saints. (101)

Rabia was "born in humble circumstances and sold into slavery as a child." (102) She was later freed by her owner, and became an ascetic of Basra, a town in Iraq. This, at least, was the standard conception developing in hagiological sources. The truth is that very little is really known about her. "Even though she most certainly existed as a historical figure, her personality is wrapped in later stories that are impossible to substantiate." (103) She is often credited with introducing the theme of divine love into the teaching of early ascetic circles in Islam.

Other female ascetics of the early period were mentioned in the tenth century report by Sulami (d. 1021) of Nishapur. His *Memorial of Female Sufis* gives an insight into the number of women who were ascetics and traditionists associated with the increasingly popular Sufism. (104) By comparison with famous male Sufis, these women are relatively little known.

The position of women in Islamic countries deteriorated during the third century after the death of Prophet Muhammad. This development has been attributed to the increasing codification of Quranic tradition by the canonists of an emerging legalism, who inflexibly applied their interpretation of early Arabian social conditions to non-Arab milieux which had been absorbed by military conquests. (105)

There is a difficulty in finding references to women in well-known works like Hujwiri's *Kashf al-Mahjub*, a Persian Sufi classic of the eleventh century. Even Rabia is absent here from the lists of Sufi saints, so overwhelmingly masculine in componency. Instead Rabia appears in an anecdote, encompassing a few lines only, in a supplementary chapter. (106) How much fact is involved in the hagiologies is a pertinent question. Sufism became assimilable to orthodox religion, which desired Sufis in a format acceptable to the legalists and *ulama*.

In the fifteenth century, the Persian poet Jami of Herat (d. 1492) composed an extensive work called *Nafahat al-Uns (Breezes of Intimacy)*. This listed over 560 male Sufis and related figures, with the addition of 34 entries on female saints. Jami's *Nafahat* is described as "the classic Persian *tadhkira* [compendium] of Sufi and Sufi-affiliated saintly figures" (Lawrence 1993, p. 23). The ratio of 17:1 may be considered significant.

A twelfth century entity was Fatima bint Ibn al-Muthanna, one of the female teachers of the famous Muhyiuddin Ibn al-Arabi (d. 1240), who lived in Spain. Fatima was an ascetic over ninety years old, and reputedly possessed a "pink and fresh" complexion. She lived at Seville, in a situation of "extreme poverty, feeding herself from the waste that the people of Seville left outside their doors." (107) She apparently had no home until Ibn al-Arabi and two other of her disciples constructed a reed hut for her use. There is some comparison possible with the instance of Babajan.

"Sufism, more than stern orthodoxy, offered women a certain amount of possibilities to participate actively in the religious and social life." (108)

In later medieval times, the sources give details of convents where women could gather under Sufi auspices. In Mamluk Egypt, such convents were led by a female preceptor (*shaykha*). However, there was nothing similar to orders of nuns as known in Christian Europe. A number of dervish orders had women affiliated to them as lay members. This marginal role was accentuated by some conservative orders via a prohibition against women entering the sanctuaries. (109)

One dervish order granted distinctive freedom for women. This was the Bektashiyya of Ottoman Turkey. (110) In this unusual grouping, the women were "absolutely equal with men," participating in the same initiation ceremony, the same gatherings, and communal meals. That egalitarianism evoked accusations of immorality against the Bektashis from the insular clerics of Turkey. (111) The Bektashiyya were one of the dervish orders disbanded by the new modernist government of Kemal Ataturk in 1925.

Relevant is the role of women in sponsoring Sufi activities. Affluent women of goodwill contributed to social service and the founding of *khanaqahs* (dervish centres). Many tomb shrines in Turkey, North Africa, India, and Pakistan attest to the existence of women saints, who mostly survive only in legend. There are even shrines to which men are not admitted. "It is remarkable that, in modern times Sufi teaching is, to a large extent, carried on by women." (112).

Amongst those who escaped oblivion were two figures of royal background in Mughal India. The princess Jahanara (1614–81) was the daughter of the Mughal emperor Shah Jahan. The Persian treatise *Dabistan-i Mazahib* referred to this woman in glowing terms as having gained spiritual knowledge by following instructions of the Qadiri teacher Mulla Shah Badakshi, a Sufi *pir* who was a mentor to the liberal prince Dara Shikoh. (113)

Jahanara was a year older than her brother Dara Shikoh (1615–59), to whom she was far more partial than her doctrinaire brother Aurangzeb. She became the pupil of Mulla Shah Badakshi in 1640-1, at the same period as Shikoh. She was formally initiated into the Qadiri order of dervishes; however, there was no question of her gaining recognition as a member of any dervish hierarchy. The protocol was too male-oriented in these widespread Sufi orders.

"Mulla Shah led a very simple and unostentatious life of poverty. No servants were kept, no meals were cooked, and no lamps were lighted in his house... he used to sit in darkness.... Mulla Shah was one of the most eminent Qadiri teachers in India. A man of culture and refined literary tastes, he was himself a scholar and a poet of no mean distinction. As a mystic he was very outspoken and unconventional in his utterances.... As a liberal thinker, he believed in the fundamental uniformity of all religious beliefs." (114)

Jahanara was originally an adherent of the Chishti order, and wrote a biography of the well-known Chishti saint Khwaja Moinuddin Chishti (d. 1236), who had lived in an earlier era. In another work, she indicated the difficulties that she found in contacting contemporary Chishti *shaikhs*. "I am devoted to the Chishti order, and although at the present time, there are great Chishti saints alive, they prefer to live in a state of seclusion." (115) Her brother Dara recommended Mulla Shah, and so she transferred allegiance to the Qadiri exponent. Dara Shikoh persuaded Mulla Shah to accept Jahanara as a disciple. She met the Sufi twice and received occasional letters from him.

According to Jahanara's own statement, she was the first woman in the house of Timur (from whom the Mughals were descended) to take in interest in Sufi matters. She was a loyal supporter of her brother Dara Shikoh in a conflict for the throne, and unsuccessfully attempted to persuade Aurangzeb (1618–1707) to surrender. The latter hated his elder brother.

A war of succession occurred after the emperor Shah Jahan became ill in 1657. He was then in the care of his favourite son Dara Shikoh, whose prominence was resented by his three brothers. Aurangzeb outwitted Shikoh, and besieged his father at Agra in 1658, placing the emperor under arrest. Shah Jahan was imprisoned in the Agra fort, and was attended by Jahanara. Aurangzeb eliminated all his brothers, and gained the throne, assuming the title of *alamgir* (conqueror of the world). His ascendancy was thereafter glorified in conservative annals.

Shikoh has often been depicted by his critics as an introverted mystic, incapable of matching Aurangzeb in military strategy. This episode requires due examination. After suffering military defeats, Shikoh attempted an escape to Iran via Sind. He made the mistake of trusting an Afghan general whose life he had previously saved. Malik Jiwan controlled the Dadar fortress near the Bolan Pass, and proved treacherous, hoping to gain a reward from Aurangzeb. As a consequence, Shikoh and his son were escorted to Delhi.

At the command of Aurangzeb, the two prisoners were paraded through the streets in chains. They were further humiliated by appearing in tattered garments while seated on an inferior elephant. Some citizens of Delhi are reported by an eye-witness (Bernier) to have wept at the sight, lamenting that nobody came forward to defend Shikoh, who had gained a reputation for compassion. However, some of Malik Jiwan's Afghan soldiers were attacked and wounded by supporters of Shikoh, who rallied at this juncture.

The counter-demonstration of public support spurred the decision of Aurangzeb to execute Shikoh and his son, who were consigned to prison. Aurangzeb arranged an assembly of hostile clergy and noblemen, who declared Shikoh to be an apostate from Islam. In 1659, Dara Shikoh was executed "not only on charges of heresy and infidelity, but for the crime of calling Hinduism and Islam 'twin brothers.' " (116)

The conservative reaction of the *ulama* was aroused by the liberalism of Shikoh, whose distinctive work *Majma al-Bahrain* (*Confluence of the Two Oceans*) was devoted to the convergence between Sufism and Vedanta. Shikoh had studied the *Upanishads*, and recently supervised a Persian translation of these (and other) Hindu texts. In theory at least, this liberal move into comparative religion could have solved many social problems. Yet orthodox chronicles like the *Alamgir-Nama* (a record of Aurangzeb) took the attitude that Hindu learned men were "worthless teachers of delusions" to be shunned (Hasrat 1982, p. 221). The cultural divide was enforced by religious insularism.

The ruthless new monarch was also opposed to the gnostic *wahdat al-wujud* teachings of Mulla Shah Badakshi (d. 1661), who was now in danger. Jahanara urged her brother Aurangzeb to adopt a more reasonable attitude in that direction, and is thought to have been instrumental in saving the life of the Sufi.

At the time of the new emperor's coronation, Mulla Shah tactfully composed a poem to commemorate the event. Aurangzeb grasped that the Sufi could not be eliminated on grounds of violating the religious law, and also knew that a persecution of Sufi subscribers to *wahdat al-wujud* was potentially disruptive (there were too many of them by that time). Instead, he condemned Mulla Shah for a grave error, meaning that of discussing wujudi teachings with the supplanted emperor Shah Jahan. Aurangzeb could here invoke the Sufi proviso that these teachings should only be discussed in the private assemblies of informed dervishes.

Mulla Shah was ordered to move from Kashmir to Lahore, within easy access of the court. There he lived and died in discreet seclusion, attended by one of Jahanara's servants. However, he is also reported to have expressed ecstatic utterances on the subject of *wahdat al-wujud*, ignoring advice to restrain himself in such afflicted times.

When the confined Shah Jahan died in 1666, Aurangzeb became reconciled to Jahanara, whom he had regarded with suspicion because of her support for Shikoh and Shah Jahan. She became part of Aurangzeb's court at the end of her life. She never married. (117)

At the time of Jahanara's death, the puritanical monarch had recently reimposed the hated *jizya* tax upon his Hindu subjects. This zealous tactic of 1679 did not work to his ultimate advantage. The afflicting tax caused a revolt amongst his Rajput subjects, and these events alienated his son, the Prince Muhammad Akbar.

Aurangzeb's daughter Zebunnisa also encountered problems. She unfortunately reaped much obscurity; her biographical details are scattered, and not in any connected form. One deduction has been that no court chronicler dared to speak of her, this princess being in disfavour with Aurangzeb during her later years.

Born in 1638, from her childhood Zebunnisa showed marked intelligence. She learned Arabic in four years, and acquired proficiency in mathematics and astronomy. Aurangzeb prevented her from continuing to write a commentary on the *Quran*; the reason may have been because the views she expressed were unorthodox. In addition to the sciences, she was also dexterous at poetry; her father was averse to poetry, and she had to write in secret. She reputedly wrote to many learned men of her time and maintained discussions with them.

Zebunnisa was devoted to her uncle Dara Shikoh, from whom she may have acquired some of her unorthodox ideas. In the long term, the most likely source of influence was her aunt Jahanara, who has been viewed as providing an example of scholarship and Sufi ideals.

Zebunnisa did not share the narrow orthodoxy of her father. She has been classified as a Sufi of the more liberal type. Much of her personal allowance was apparently deployed to encourage men of the pen, to provide for widows and orphans, and to aid poor pilgrims in travelling to Mecca on the pilgrimage (*hajj*). Zebunnisa accumulated a well-stocked library, and patronised a scriptorium in Kashmir where scribes and calligraphers exercised their skills. She had a number of learned works translated from Arabic into Persian; Arabic was not spoken by all Muslims in India.

At an uncertain date, Zebunnisa was despatched by her father to the fortress prison of Salimgarh, located at Delhi. There she stayed for twenty years until her death. The reasons are not clear, and various theories have been formulated concerning this tragic event. Perhaps the most convincing explanation is that she was in liaison with her brother Muhammad Akbar, the prince who revolted against Aurangzeb. Akbar maintained that his insularist father was unfit to rule, and even crowned himself as emperor, before being outmanoeuvred.

Aurangzeb moved his court south to Aurangabad in the Deccan, and personally assumed command of the Deccan campaign. Every year he sent armies against the Marathas, aggressively plundering and burning villages. In 1685, thousands of Muslim rebels proclaimed the Prince Akbar as emperor, but he failed to conquer Ahmednagar. The rebels were defeated, and Akbar fled to Iran, never daring to return. Aurangzeb despatched a death squad to hunt down the Maratha king Sambhaji, son and successor of Shivaji (d. 1660), who had pioneered the Maratha empire. Sambhaji was tortured and killed, but the Maratha guerrilla warfare continued.

Marek concluded that Aurangzeb tortured to death his own daughter. She died after an illness and was buried near Lahore; the date has been variously assessed from 1689 to 1702.

From this obscurity and subjection, some thirty-five years after her death, the remnants of Zebunnisa's scattered Persian poems were collected under the title of *Diwan-i-Makhfi* (Book of the Hidden One). These compositions have been described as exhibiting a Sufi style with an Indian flavour, reflecting a tradition of the unification of religions associated with her forbear, the liberal emperor Akbar (d. 1605). (118) The latter is noted for a policy of "total peace" or "peace with all" (*sulh-i kull*).

Two letters to Zebunnisa from the Naqshbandi *shaikh* Abdul Ahad (d. 1729–30) have been described as fine literary pieces, and imply that the princess had commenced the Naqshbandi discipline. (119) The attendant situation in her case is obscure.

Abdul Ahad was a figurehead of the Mujaddidiyya sect, an offshoot of the Naqshbandi order, which had much older origins. He was a grandson of Ahmad (Faruqi) Sirhindi (d. 1624), the proclaimed *mujaddid* (reviver of Islam). The Mujaddidiya exercised a strong hereditary profile. This zealous Sunni grouping advocated the suppression of Hindus, and were markedly hostile towards Shia Muslims. They detested the liberal policy of the emperor Akbar. They also resisted the teaching of *wahdat al-wujud,* instead preferring the compatibility with orthodoxy represented by Sirhindi's *wahdat al-shuhud.* (120)

The teachings of Sirhindi were banned in 1679, when influential *ulama* opposed the extravagances of spiritual prerogative claimed by Sirhindi in his letters. Meanwhile, the various grandsons of Sirhindi were active as exponents of his teaching, a situation exhibiting internal rivalries. This controversial sect gained enthusiasts via a process of hagiological inflation. (121)

In 1666, Aurangzeb was apparently initiated into the Naqshbandi order shortly before the death of Shah Jahan. This induction reputedly occurred via Shaikh Muhammad Masum, the son and successor of Sirhindi, (122) and more especially Masum's son Saifuddin (d. 1685), another prominent Mujaddidi representative. Saifuddin infiltrated the court at Delhi, with the objective of transmitting to Aurangzeb the Naqshbandi discipline. This exponent also wished to promote Sunni Islam and oppose the Shi'is. Saifuddin wrote many letters to the monarch, and also other prestigious persons. One of these letters, addressed to the Sultan Abdur-Rahman, is solely concerned with advocating miraculous cures, purportedly acquired by drinking water in which the slippers of Ahmad Sirhindi (the Mujaddid) had been immersed (Rizvi 1983, p. 486).

Three letters of Muhammad Masum to his son Saifuddin, who lived at the court of Aurangzeb, "suggest that both the father and the son considered Aurangzeb had attained a very high spiritual status in the mystical hierarchy" (Rizvi 1983, p. 5). The Sufi "spiritual hierarchy" is here meant. If Aurangzeb believed in this form of status, any objector might have been a candidate for censure, his daughter included.

Although the Mujaddidi sect appears to have gained a strong foothold at the Mughal court during the 1660s, (123) one version is that "they did not play any part in influencing the political or economic policy of the Emperor [Aurangzeb]." (124) The same informed scholar contended that the chaos prevalent among Indian Muslims during the lengthy reign of Aurangzeb exposed the shallowness of Ahmad Sirhindi's contention that all evils could be removed if only the rulers could be converted to [Sunni] orthodoxy." (125)

The new scholarship revealed that, contrary to hagiology, any revitalising of Muslim society during the reign of Aurangzeb and his successors, was the outcome of efforts made by the supporters of *wahdat al-wujud* and the attendant policy of "peace with all." The wujudi monistic philosophy had a wider appeal in India than in any other part of the Islamic world. The popularity of this teaching continued during the reign of Aurangzeb, despite the latter's conservatism. Indeed, the wujudi spirit served to inspire the Muslim population in North India until the mid-nineteenth century, when British imperialism altered the balance. (126)

The constant insularist warfare of Aurangzeb did not prove to be a victory, but instead contributed to a persisting turmoil. Eager to extend the boundaries of his empire, he formed an extensive army, which exhausted his prodigious wealth. Aurangzeb alienated the Sikhs, and anarchy developed amongst Pathans on the north-west frontier. The biggest drawback was his war in the Deccan, lasting for more than twenty years. His military camp has been described as a city of tents, extending for about thirty miles, and swallowing up surplus grain, a problem which caused famine in the Deccan. The situation was aggravated by plague.

Despite the huge loss in lives, and the enormous expense, there was no resolution of the political deadlock. The oppressed Marathas refused to submit. During the last years of his life, Aurangzeb regularly besieged and conquered forts, but the Marathas continually regained their territories. Aurangzeb died at Ahmednagar, and was buried unpretentiously at Khuldabad, in the grounds of a Chishti Sufi shrine, where his memory gained sanctity. (127)

In his last years, Aurangzeb wrote in a letter: "Most of the country has been rendered desolate." (128) He blamed this setback upon the infidels, but a different conclusion is possible. When political subjects are overtaxed and stigmatised, and conditions of war prevail, problems will accumulate.

The ruination and affliction was widely perceived. In 1687, a severe famine and cholera epidemic occurred when the Deccan cities of Bijapur and Golconda were conquered by Aurangzeb. At Masulipatnam, the death toll was estimated at 500,000 by the European commentator Daniel Havart. The situation in Masulipatnam was so chronic that some inhabitants hoped to be saved from starvation by going into slavery. A few years after the conquest of Bijapur, a Mughal census revealed that the city had lost over half the population.

The Deccani Sufi poet Mahmud Bahri witnessed the fall of Bijapur, and became a recluse in his native town of Gogi. He fled because his unorthodox form of Sufism was investigated by a hostile *qazi* (legist) "who was purging the city on behalf of the new government," and who had already killed one Sufi for making utterances contrary to Islamic law. (129)

The consequences of martial strife were enduring. The first recorded riot between Hindus and Muslims occurred in 1714 at Ahmedabad. (130) The Mughal rulers lost their ascendancy during the eighteenth century, and a resulting power vacuum was filled, at first by the punitive Marathas and Afghans, and afterwards by the colonial British. Neither the Hindus nor the Muslims were victors.

Two centuries after Aurangzeb, Hazrat Babajan demonstrated a strong tangent to the aristocratic role, thus evading the attendant subjection suffered by Jahanara and Zebunnisa. She rigorously adopted the *faqir* lifestyle, renouncing all wealth, servants, and status. The Pathan mystic was in affinity with the monistic perspective of *wahdat al-wujud*, but remained unconcerned with any systematisation of that teaching. Babajan can be described as an unusual *faqir* and neo-*qalandar*, living completely outside the Sufi orders favoured by orthodoxy and royalty. Her political profile being nil, Babajan nevertheless became famous in British Raj Poona, the public response to her funeral serving to prove her impact.

Appendix 1:
Drawbacks in Miracle Lore

𝒯he late Dr. Marianne Warren (d. 2004) authored a book on Shirdi Sai Baba (d. 1918). That work makes a valid contribution to the subject, serving to confirm the Sufi background of Shirdi Sai. The exposition is attended by uncritical references to "miracles." Dr. Warren was strongly influenced by the miracle lore attaching to Sathya Sai Baba (d. 2011), having become a devotee of that controversial guru. She became very disillusioned with Sathya Sai shortly after her book was published in 1999; a subsequent revised edition did not alter the basic text.

Dr. Warren included three pages on Babajan in her book. She neglected to mention my own work *A Sufi Matriarch: Hazrat Babajan* (1986), the only annotated book on the subject. I was in some disfavour as a critic of Sathya Sai Baba, and solely because of a brief reference in another early work of mine. Academic selectivity is questionable when sectarian biases are implicated. To avoid further confusion, I will here quote the passage that caused disfavour (but which pleased the Shirdi Sai contingent):

"Some of [Shirdi] Sai Baba's latter day following have a grievance with which it is easy to sympathise. This relates to the claims made for a certain namesake of the original Sai Baba, who encourages an obsession with wonder-working and is believed to be the avataric reincarnation of the Shirdi saint. The more critical Hindus deem this sort of occurrence to be amusingly theatrical, but it is more serious when historical studies are affected adversely by popular gullibility." (*Gurus Rediscovered,* pp. 1–2)

According to Dr. Warren, the career of Babajan has "striking points of similarity with [Shirdi] Sai Baba in terms of lifestyle and miraculous powers" (Warren 1999, p. 200). In terms of lifestyle, yes, but powers are a very misleading subject. Dr. Warren is ten years out in attributing the incident of Baluchi *sepoys* to the commencement of Babajan's sojourn in Poona.

"For the next thirty years or more she lived under the *neem* tree in Char Bavadi, where she gave *darshan,* accepting only tea from devotees, and occasionally performing some miracle of healing" (ibid., p. 200).

There are three errors in that statement, even leaving out the attribution of miracle healing. Babajan spent twenty years in Char Bavadi, and did accept a variety of other gifts, including food and items of clothing (which she had a habit of quickly redistributing). *Darshan* is a Hindu term, and associated with the reverential homage occurring in the company of Hindu saints and gurus. There was no such procedure with Babajan, who was averse to anyone bowing down to her.

The same academic insists that "the few recorded miracles she [Babajan] performed are extraordinarily similar to those of [Shirdi] Sai Baba." Here a difference looms, however. There follows the statement:

"Unlike Sai Baba, Babajan did not have an apostle-type scribe like Narasimhaswami to interview all the people who came to see her and collect their experiences; however, Meher Baba did record a few and Dr. A. G. Munsiff also recorded a number. In total these miraculous events constitute a twelve-page booklet which serves as her biography" (Warren 1999, p. 201).

In reality, Meher Baba did not record any miracle experiences. The scribe was Dr. Abdul Ghani (pen name Munsiff), who authored the collection which is referred to. There is no 12-page booklet on those events, but instead an early article of Ghani supplementing his biographical article. Both of those articles were much later reprinted in a 72-page booklet published by Meher Baba devotees, along with other materials. The title page attributed the contents to Meher Baba and Dr. Ghani, a factor which evidently misled Dr. Warren. The general muddle in this subject is disconcerting. Cf. the qualifying reference in Shepherd, *Investigating the Sai Baba Movement*, 2005, pp. 54–55.

The deference of Dr. Warren to the "apostle-type scribe" Narasimhaswami resulted in another discrepancy. The present writer was rebuked by Dr. Warren for being "very opinionated" in dismissing Narasimhaswami as an "opportunist" (Warren 1999, p. 24 note 38). She failed to understand that my remarks about B. V. Narasimhaswami in *Gurus Rediscovered* (1986) were directly derived from Meher Baba, who strongly disagreed with the miracle lore dominant at Shirdi, a lore strongly influenced by Narasimhaswami. Dr. Warren ignored my tangible references in this respect (Shepherd 1986, pp. 3–4). She instead erroneously opted to depict Meher Baba as the joint author of Ghani's *Miracles of Babajan*. Shortly after, Dr. Warren discovered with dismay that the alleged miracleworker Sathya Sai Baba had evoked severe criticism of an undesirable kind from his own former devotees. She herself became an ex-devotee.

At large, the media situation is still discrepant with regard to Hazrat Babajan. For instance, the Internet has displayed an item describing Babajan as a philosopher. In reality, she was an intuitive mystic and *faqir*. For years, Wikipedia has been describing Babajan as "a Baloch Muslim saint," causing confusions by ignoring the Pathan identity.

Appendix 2:

Differences in Subject Coverage

*T*he procedure in representing Hazrat Babajan has varied from the devotional to the critical. Unfortunately, the latter recourse has opted for a misrepresentation. The influence of Babajan in the Char Bavadi area of Poona cantonment quite quickly resulted in the renovation of a slum precinct, and also the cessation of criminal tendencies in that locale. Yet she is unjustly implied by a Western male critic as being part of the drug den she and her devotees eliminated. A grave misconception is evident in Nile Green's *Islam and the Army in Colonial India* (2009, pp. 128ff).

The superficial judgment asserts that Babajan "had become a kind of mad hostess for the cantonment's low-life's soirees" (ibid., p. 130). The misunderstanding evidenced by such statements is pronounced; Green fails to give relevant details of the 1910–1931 period, instead substituting a fiction. A considerable insult is thereby extended to hundreds of Muslim devotees, Pathan and Baluchi soldiers, Zoroastrians, and others.

The negative angle in this version is so extreme that even the name of the subject is given an aspersive complexion. Green favours the translation of "Babajan" in terms of "dear child," and supports this preference with the generalising statement that *faqirs* were "innocent, trusting and wonderstruck but, at the same time fickle, vengeful and capricious" (ibid., p. 128). This sounds too poetic for analysts who desire the history of the subject as distinct from superimposed rhetorical deliberations.

In similar idiom is the adverse reflection that "all of the accounts of Baba Jan present her in the same guise of holy fool as Bane Miyan, raving and muttering, prone to caprice and eccentricity" (ibid., p. 131). Again a stress on caprice, be it noted. Careful reading of all the accounts (including my own former book on the subject) should result in a different interpretation. The accusations of Professor Green are glossed by other suggestions of his, such as:

> "It was the image of the *faqir* as trickster, ever able to slip out of trouble or pull a card from their sleeves at the very moment that they – or their clients – needed it" (ibid.).

This very confusing comment was in extension of the burial alive episode occurring in North India (see Chapter 8). The situation is that of an elderly woman consigned to a premature grave by implacable fundamentalists. Yet in Western "holy fool" lore, the reported escape is merely a subject of trickster image significance associated with supposed clients. In this instance, the "clients" were Baluchi *sepoys* who perpetrated the crime, and who subsequently reported their misdeed. Babajan did not seek their attention. These soldiers happened to arrive at her tree in Char Bavadi, and there recognised her from the past. They were not clients, but spectators. Some of them reputedly became devotees, a word not understood by all Western academics.

The exegesis of "holy fool," incorporating the fashionable neo-Jungian cliché of "trickster," amounts to a conflation, subtraction, and diversion. The "holy fool" theory even employs reference to a nineteenth century "house of ill repute," frequented by soldiers at another cantonment in India. The misleading "holy fool" mythology would do better to stay within the bounds of relevant twentieth century facts. Nile Green presents the Pathan *sepoys* of the Poona cantonment as revellers, a forced interpretation which moves at a distinct tangent to the known details.

The *majzub* Bane Miyan (d. 1921) of Aurangabad is largely visible only through a hagiography of doubtful accuracy. In contrast, the instance of Hazrat Babajan has some solid historical ballast, and indeed more so than most other records of Eastern female mystics. Ironically, this testament is in danger of being eliminated in a manner that might easily be considered capricious.

Almost incidentally, one may observe that the "holy fool" theory assigns Babajan to a chapter entitled *Allah's naked rebels*. The fact is that she was always fully clothed, observing due modesty. Trickster lore in the West can be deceptive via juxtapositions and inappropriate judgments.

Misrepresentation of a subject is always to be lamented, and perhaps especially in the instance of a woman who provided an alternative angle to inflexible doctrines of the *ulama* and also the British colonial mindset.

It is strongly arguable that coverages which miss out relevant details are in basic error. Superficial judgments can obscure much of the context in any biography. It is surely better to adopt a more empathic approach, allowing due focus upon the details suppressed in facile/hostile coverage.

Hazrat Babajan maintained a lifestyle of *faqir* health that resisted medication and drugs to the end. She could quickly recover from fever and illness that might leave other people prostrate for much longer. She knew the difference between health and addiction, and is known to have greatly benefited her environment in Poona.

I will repeat here the observation that Babajan "had an aversion to artificial methods and applications, and appears to have regarded European medicine with the same circumspection as she did the hemp and opium of the local drug addicts" (Shepherd 1986, p. 68).

There is no sect or movement adhering to Babajan. Her tomb has gained veneration as a pilgrimage site, but no doctrinal or organisational vehicle is in evidence. She

Pathan Native Officer, Punjab 1858

**Sir Winston Churchill as subaltern in the
4th Hussars, 1895**

The Old Pathan
(*The National Geographic Magazine*, 1921)

Afridi Pathan warriors, undated

Afridi Pathan officer and sepoys, Khyber Rifles, 1895

Sir Richard Burton   Hazrat Babajan at Poona (Meelan Photo Studio, Pune)

Baluchi soldiers, Baluch 26th Regiment, 1897   Dr. Abdul Ghani

Hazrat Tajuddin
Baba of Nagpur

Sheriar Mundegar Irani,
Poona, 1890s

Merwan S. Irani
(Meher Baba), 1913

Meher Baba, 1929

Gustad Hansotia, 1922

Mehera J. Irani

M.R. Dhakephalkar

Paul Brunton in India

is sometimes associated with the Meher Baba movement, due to the fact that she exercised a strong influence upon the figurehead. Yet that influence was not of a doctrinal nature. The present writer is not a member of any movement, adopting a neutral stance in this respect.

Notes

(1) Ghani, "Hazrat Babajan of Poona" (1939), p. 31. This was the earliest biography, and written several years after the subject's death by the medic Dr. Abdul Ghani (who had also served as a small-time magistrate or *munsiff*, a vocational title often mistaken for his surname). Ghani was an Indian Muslim. His compact account was later reprinted in *The Awakener* (1961), 8 (1): 12-22. Another reprint was included in M. R. Kantak, ed., *Hazrat Babajan* (1981). Dr. Kantak, of the Deccan College (Poona), was only mentioned on the acknowledgment page (page 6) by the publisher K. K. Ramakrishnan, who was secretary for the Meher Baba Centre in Poona. This booklet caused confusion in the case of Dr. Marianne Warren, because the varied contents of that publication were attributed on the title page to Meher Baba and Dr. Ghani. As a consequence, a contribution by Ghani was mistakenly identified with Meher Baba's joint authorship by Dr. Warren. "This is an instance of how the appetite for miracles can distort the record in basic respects, leading to potentially serious problems for later researchers" (Shepherd, *Investigating the Sai Baba Movement*, 2005, p. 55). See also Appendice One in the present book.

(2) Ghani, article cited in note 1, p. 31. In this context, Dr. Ghani described his account in terms of "the most authenticated version as yet presented to the world." The derivative report of Jean Adriel followed Ghani, asserting that "Babajan was born in Afghanistan of well-to-do, aristocratic Mohammedan parentage" (Adriel 1947, p. 36).

(3) C. B. Purdom, *The Perfect Master* (1937), p. 19. Purdom was here repeating what he had been told by Indian devotees of Meher Baba, who was the main subject of his book. I met Purdom in 1965, and found him to be an unusually analytical follower of Meher Baba, one who did not always trust devotional reports. On Purdom, see further: Shepherd, *Meher Baba, an Iranian Liberal* (1988), pp. 190ff.

(4) Shepherd, *Hazrat Babajan, a Pathan (Pashtun) Sufi* (online article). Earlier, I made a concession to the Purdom version by stating that the birth of Babajan "appears to have occurred in Baluchistan, probably on its borders near Quetta" (*A Sufi Matriarch: Hazrat Babajan*, 1986, p. 27). Today, Quetta is in West Pakistan, but was originally part of the Afghan domain. Reference to Baluchistan as the birthplace can suggest an attribution, drawn from associations with the era of British annexation, still dominant at the time when Purdom was writing. However, the word "Balochistan" does occur in early British reports of India (e.g. the 1840s travel narrative of Charles Masson). The basic point is that, in the case of Babajan, reference to Baluchistan can be confusing with regard to ethnic definition. This confusion led to Babajan being described on Wikipedia as "a Baloch Muslim saint," an error still promoted at the time of writing.

(5) The weavings of Baluchi women have caused surprise that nineteenth-century British travellers gave a totally disproportionate attention to Baluchi weapons (although the now well-known Baluchi rugs are associated with Iranian regions rather than Baluchistan). See R. Kossow in D. Black and C. Loveless, *Rugs of the Wandering Baluchi* (1976), p. 9, observing that after more than 1,800 pages of text, Charles Masson expressed not a word of praise for the quality of design found in Baluchi weaving. See further Masson, *Narrative of Various Journeys in Balochistan, Afghanistan, and the Punjab* (4 vols, 1842–4). For Baluchi weavings, see Jeff W, Boucher, *Baluchi Woven Treasures* (1996), p. 14, who says

that Baluchi pile rugs are chiefly associated with the Iranian province of Khorasan, and also the vicinity of Zabol in Sistan. Whereas "the tribes of Baluchistan weave only flat-woven items and a few pile items" which are generally unattractive. Many of the antique rugs featured in the plates of Boucher come from Khorasan, and so Masson might not have seen weavings of that type. Some associated antique weavings, such as Timuri rugs, come from north-west Afghanistan. With regard to Baluchi origins, see R. N. Frye, "Remarks on Baluchi History," (1961), informing that the earliest historical accounts are found in the Arabic geographies of the tenth century CE. At the time of the Arab conquest of Iran, it is here inferred, the Baluchis were living in the region of Kerman. They apparently moved eastward during the eleventh and twelfth centuries, spreading throughout Makran and Sistan, and probably entered Sind during the Mongol era. Two later movements of Baluchi tribes to Khorasan have been discussed, starting with the reputed removal of a Baluch population to Khorasan from Baluchistan by Nadir Shah in the eighteenth century. See also R. N. Frye, "Baluchistan," in *The Encyclopaedia of Islam Vol. 1* (new edn., Leiden, 1960). Another ethnic complexity of Baluchistan is the tribal people known as Brahui, united in the eighteenth century under the leadership of Nasir Khan, who ruled most areas of Baluchistan, and who fought against the Afghan monarch Ahmad Shah Abdali, to whom he surrendered. The Afghans then ruled much of Baluchistan. Many Brahui tribes were later assimilated by the Baluch, and identities were sometimes anomalous, even Nasir Khan being described as a Baluchi by posterity. In the 1901 census, the Baluchi population in the Persian zone of Baluchistan was estimated at 250,000, while British Baluchistan harboured some 300,000. About the same number of Brahui lived in British Baluchistan. A large number of Baluchi people also existed by that time in Sind and Punjab. See Siawosch Azadi, *Carpets in the Baluch Tradition* (1986), pp. 17–18, 34–6. Also of interest is M. Longworth Dames, *The Baloch Race* (1904). On the ascendant Baluchis in Sind, see Burton, *Sindh and the Races* (1851), pp. 236ff.

(6) Purdom, *op. cit.*, p. 115. Charles Purdom also wrote his autobiography *Life over Again* (1951). His adherence to Meher Baba is notable for some unusual perspectives. For instance, see Purdom. "What I Understand Baba's Teachings to Be," *The Awakener* (1958) 5 (2): 4-7. "We cannot really talk about Baba's teaching, for unless it changes our lives inwardly, it does not exist for us" (ibid., p. 5)." Further, "the idea that Baba intends to perform some sensational act in the world is a great error" (ibid., p. 6).

(7) J. J. Roy Burman, *Hindu-Muslim Syncretic Shrines and Communities* (2002), p. 237. Professor Burman is here relaying an oral source. Babajan "is said to be the daughter of one Bahadur Shah Zaffar and had come from Afghanistan" (ibid.).

(8) For the early reigns in the Afghan empire, see *The History of Afghanistan – Fayz Muhammad Katib Hazarah's Siraj al-Tawarikh Vols I and 2* (2012). On the Pathans, still useful is Olaf Caroe, *The Pathans* (1958). The Pathan origins have been a subject for debate. They themselves have sometimes claimed descent from the Hebrew race, regarding Saul as their ancestor. The general consensus of scholastic opinion has assigned them to Turko-Iranian stock. The strongly aquiline Pathan facial features are frequently accompanied by clear blue eyes, a genetic trait traceable to Iranian immigrants who accompanied the invading Mughal armies. The traditional sources for the pre-Islamic Pathan phase are in Persian, and compiled at the Mughal court not earlier than the start of the seventeenth century. Caroe concluded that the Pathans ethnically represent a diversified group of peoples.

(9) Shepherd, *A Sufi Matriarch* (1986), p. 28. The *Quran* is approximately the size of the Christian New Testament. The memorisation feat seems to have varied, not necessarily applying to the entire text. Western sceptics affirmed that many of the memorisers became deficient in thinking capacity as a consequence of the attention given to this religious exercise. The exercise was favoured by the *ulama*, the religious scholars.

(10) Ibid., pp. 28–9.

(11) Ibid., p. 29. This suggestion basically arose because of the subsequent move of Gul-rukh to Peshawar, a city much closer to Kabul than to Quetta or Kandahar.

(12) Ibid.

(13) Ibid., p. 30, and citing J. A. Subhan, *Sufism, Its Saints and Shrines* (1938; repr. 1970), pp. 2–3, apparently describing a twentieth century scene in Lahore. The author of this pioneering work on Indian Sufism (which contains numerous errors) was a Methodist minister who described himself as an ex-member of the Qadiri order.

(14) Thomas Barfield, *Afghanistan: A Cultural and Political History* (2010), p. 5. On the reign of Abdur-Rahman Khan, see also Hazarah, *The History of Afghanistan Vol. 3* (2012).

(15) Percival Spear, *A History of India Vol. 2* (1970), p. 135. The Sikh empire dates to 1799–1849, and for which see Grewal, *The Sikhs of the Punjab* (1991), pp. 99ff. See also Bikrama Jit Hasrat, *Life and Times of Ranjit Singh: A Saga of Benevolent Despotism* (1977); Singh, Khushwant, A History of the Sikhs Vol. 1, First edn (2 vols, New Jersey: Princeton University Press, 1963, , pp. 196ff); second edn (New Delhi: OUP, 2004-5); Patwant Singh, *Empire of the Sikhs: The Life and Times of Maharaja Ranjit Singh* (2008).

(16) Bhau Kalchuri, *Lord Meher Vol. One* (1986) p. 9. Kalchuri merely says "recorded to be called Maula Shah," without supplying any source. His chapter on Babajan appears in the English translation of the Hindi work *Meher Prabhu*. The style is devotional, and rather poetic in idiom. Kalchuri barely mentions the Pathan background, and his basic concern was evidently to portray Babajan as a forerunner of Meher Baba. He refers to "the supremely magnificent role for which she alone was destined – to summon the Awakener to earth" (ibid.). There are disadvantages with this form of

commentary. However, Kalchuri does supply some details not found in Ghani.

(17) The phrase "God-realization" reflects the terminology of Meher Baba, who used it in the context of a very rare achievement. The Persian term *majzub* (Arabic: *majdhub*) gained popularity, and was employed rather diversely in Sufism. One usage is reflected in the phrase: "when 'possessed' (*majdhub*) he [the Sufi] was not responsible for his words and actions, he could do and say things which could be blasphemous if said by others" (Trimingham, *The Sufi Orders in Islam*, 1971, p. 150). Less dramatically, "the *majdhub* (enraptured one), a familiar aspect of traditional Islamic society, is regarded as having lost his personal consciousness in the divine Oneness" (ibid., p. 165). Meher Baba used the word *majzub* far more exactingly, to designate a rare category of "God-realized" person; his terminology had not gained definitive exposition at the time Ghani wrote the monograph on Hazrat Babajan.

(18) Purdom, *The Perfect Master*, p. 115.

(19) Purdom, *The God-Man*, p. 18. According to Ghani, article cited, p. 38, Babajan was a *qutub*, an elevated role relating to "the hierarchy of saints," a vintage component of Sufi teaching. The attribution of *qutub* derives from Meher Baba. Modern scholarship has described a central Sufi belief in terms of: "From the earliest period of Sufism, saints were regarded as the invisible supports of the universe; an invisible hierarchy headed by the *qutb* or 'axis' of the world carries out the will of God in all things" (Ernst, *Eternal Garden*, 1992, pp. 10–11).

(20) Shepherd, *A Sufi Matriarch* (1986), p. 38. The theme of *fana-baqa* is generally contracted, and often applied in a theological context. "The lower forms of *baqa* have very little in common with the more advanced grades in the series." Further, "there can be no *baqa* without *fana*" (ibid., pp. 38–9).

(21) Richard F. Burton, *Sindh and the Races that Inhabit the Valley of the Indus* (1851), pp.198ff.; Fawn M. Brodie, *The Devil Drives: A Life of Sir Richard Burton* (1967), p. 68. Burton also referred to "the miraculous lie," meaning that of miracles, observing how miracle lore could so easily take root after a generation or two (*Sindh and the Races*, p. 230). See also Edward Rice, *Captain Sir Richard Francis Burton: A Biography* (1990), stating that Burton "remained a more or less faithful practitioner of Sufi teachings for the rest of his life" (ibid., p. 3). His "Sufi diploma" has been queried by some analysts. Portrayals of the controversial Richard Burton have differed in complexion. See further Dane Kennedy, *The Highly Civilised Man: Richard Burton and the Victorian World* (2005). Burton became famous in Britain because of his 1853 pilgrimage to Mecca "in the guise of a Sufi of Pathan origin" (Kennedy, p. 3).

(22) Kalchuri, *Lord Meher Vol. One*, p. 10.

(23) Such anecdotes were presented by Ghani in an article on Babajan's "miracles" in *The Meher Baba Journal*, and reprinted in Kantak, ed., *Hazrat Babajan* (1981), pp. 47ff. Confirmation of the voyage to Arabia is found in Purdom, *The Perfect Master* (1937), p. 19, whose early report relays the same date of 1903. Cf. Kalchuri, *op. cit.*, pp. 11–12, who describes this event in terms of Babajan's second pilgrimage to Mecca. The name of the steamship has also been rendered as *Haidari*. Cf. Green, *Islam and the Army in Colonial India* (2009), p. 129, informing that the 1903 voyage was reported by *The Times of India* in 1926.

(24) Shepherd, *A Sufi Matriarch*, p. 44. See also Trimingham, *The Sufi Orders in Islam*, pp. 105–6, and observing that "all religious organisations flag in their interior life, and the [dervish] orders were, as we have seen, very decadent." See also Lapidus, *A History of Islamic Societies* (1988), p. 674, informing that Abdul Aziz ibn Saud succeeded in unifying the tribes of Arabia, taking control of the Hejaz and the

Islamic holy places in 1925, while engaged in the process of establishing the boundaries of Saudi Arabia via treaties with adjacent countries.

(25) Ghani, "Hazrat Babajan of Poona," p. 33, and specifying "the Sepoys of the Baluchi Regiment, which had only recently arrived from the North." The numerical identity of the Regiment is not supplied. Cf. Burman, *Hindu-Muslim Syncretic Shrines and Communities* (2002), p. 237, who says that the Baluchi soldiers "had learnt about her in Peshawar and heard the miraculous story of her getting buried alive." There seems to be a confusion in this later version. In the extension to Ghani's early account, he refers to the North West Frontier Province as the scene of the burial, and specifying that "some of them [the Baluchi soldiers arriving at Poona] were the actual perpetrators of the tragedy," meaning the burial (quote from "Miracles of Babajan," reprinted from *The Meher Baba Journal*, in Kantak, ed., *Hazrat Babajan*, 1981, p. 57). The Frontier Province was created in 1901, a fact which may serve to date the episode of burial. An even earlier source was also explicit on this point. See Purdom, *The Perfect Master* (1937), p. 115, reporting a 1927 commentary by Meher Baba that is missing from Vol. 3 (1988) of Kalchuri's *Lord Meher*, p. 924. This version identifies the Punjab as the locale of the burial, with no reference to any town or city. The Meher Baba version refers to "certain Baluchis of a local regiment" as the aggressors. "When she came out of the living grave she went towards Bombay" (Purdom, *op. cit.*, p. 115). Purdom mentions Rawalpindi in this context (ibid., p. 20). Cf. M. R. Dhakephalkar, *A Visit to Hazrat Babajan* (online), who refers to Quetta as the scene of premature burial. Dhake Phalkar was a devotee of Meher Baba, and his visit to Babajan at Poona occurred during the 1920s. According to Dhake, the soldiers "testified that she was more than 125 years old." Perhaps this was the origin of the *circa* 1790 birth attribution.

(26) Shepherd, *A Sufi Matriarch* (1986), pp. 49–50, dating the Poona event to 1914 on the basis of an early notice, and mentioning that the locale of the burial was apparently Rawalpindi (here following Purdom). Cf. Kalchuri, *Lord Meher Vol. One*, pp. 10–11, who favours Rawalpindi. An obscure but early Hindu source referred to the Dardanelles as the destination of the Baluchi *sepoys* who arrived at Poona. However, the failed Dardanelles campaign of the British in 1915 is not associated with any of the Baluch Regiments. A confusion apparently occurred in the transmission of the 1914 Poona episode among the devotees of Meher Baba. A substantial number of the Baluchi soldiers certainly did serve in campaigns against the Ottoman Turks during the First World War. The 124th Baluchistan Infantry served in Iran and Iraq, fighting in a number of battles against the Turks, and also participating in 1918 at the decisive Battle of Megiddo in Palestine. See Shepherd, *A Sufi Matriarch*, p. 76 note 47, referring to the Hindu devotee C. V. Sampath Aiyengar of Madras, who was editor of a local periodical concerning Meher Baba. Indian civilians may easily have confused the routes and destinations of the soldiers. Gurkhas, Sikhs, and other contingents of the Indian army did participate in the Dardanelles campaign, which suffered heavy casualties.

(27) See Major General Raffiudin Ahmed, *History of the Baloch Regiment 1820-1939* (1998). The five Regiments were part of the Bombay Native Infantry. In the new format devised by Lord Kitchener in 1903, all the Bombay military units had 100 added to their numeral identification. So, for instance, the 26th Regiment became the 126th Baluchistan Infantry, and served in Aden during the First World War. During the 1890s, this Regiment had recruited Baluchis, Brahuis, Pathans, and Punjabi Muslims. The heroic Khudadad Khan was a member of the 129th Baluchis, who served in France and Belgium during the Great War, engaging the German army.

(28) Chandrika Kaul, *From Empire to Independence: The British Raj in India 1858-1947* (BBC online article, 2011).

(29) Ghani, "Hazrat Babajan of Poona," p. 35. Ghani viewed this assertion as confirmation of a *hadith* (tradition) ascribed to Muhammad: "Lovers of God are males; lovers of paradise are eunuchs; and lovers of the world are females." Women might object to the phraseology, as Babajan may well have done.

(30) Kalchuri, *Lord Meher Vol. One*, p. 13, identifying the devotee as Kasam (Kasim) V. Rafai.

(31) On this figure, see Shepherd, *Investigating the Sai Baba Movement* (2005), part one; Marianne Warren, *Unravelling the Enigma: Shirdi Sai Baba in the Light of Sufism* (1999); Shepherd, *Shirdi Sai Baba and the Sai Baba Movement* (online article).

(32) Ghani, "Hazrat Babajan of Poona," p. 35. Two well-known photographs of Babajan to some extent bear out this description. The image associated with Meelan Photo Studio underwent a degree of retouching, erasing the facial wrinkles. Cf. Burman, *Hindu-Muslim Syncretic Shrines and Communities* (2002), p. 237, who relays a contention that Babajan "used to wear dress like men and kept short hair and that is why she was called Baba Jan – a man's name." This explanation is not convincing in view of her prolific hair, and certainly not for the Poona phase. However, there might be some relevance to her earlier years and the legendary first pilgrimage to Mecca. Another commentary says that "for a while, she [Babajan] wandered around in male attire and finally settled down in Poona" (Tahera Aftab, *Inscribing South Asian Muslim Women*, 2008, p. 103).

(33) Kalchuri, *op. cit.*, p. 13, informing that the mosque of Bukhari Shah was next door to the home of Sardar Raste. Kalchuri was one of the *mandali* (resident devotees) at the ashram of Meher Baba near Ahmednagar.

(34) Kalchuri, *op. cit.*, p. 13, informing that the mother of Shaikh Imam wished to give Babajan new clothes. The saint consistently refused, but eventually agreed. "With the utmost difficulty and patience, the Shaikh's mother gently

bathed her old body and attired her in a new clean robe and undergarments especially stitched for her" (ibid.). The event is undated. According to Kalchuri, this was the last bath that Babajan was to have, although a contrasting contention has been expressed in relation to the matter. See Shepherd, *Minds and Sociocultures Vol. One* (1995), pp. 193–4 note 253, and concluding that ablutions "occurred at the homes of devotees, and not at the more conspicuous venue at the neem tree in Char Bavadi, where privacy was virtually impossible." The popular version of omitted details tended to miracle lore, in which the bodily fragrance of the matriarch was emphasised. This intricacy was overlooked in a disparaging version of Babajan, which sweepingly asserted that "in the decades after she arrived in Poona she never once washed" (Green, *Islam and the Army in Colonial India*, p. 131). I do not agree with the earlier statement of Purdom that "for twenty years before her death she did not take a bath" (*The Perfect Master*, p. 21). Purdom contributed a brief report on Babajan that lacks many details found elsewhere; for instance, he makes no mention of Shaikh Imam or his mother. I deferred to the Purdom version in *A Sufi Matriarch*, p. 69, composed in the late 1970s. My early doubts were later confirmed and reactivated by new information that had not formerly been published.

(35) Ghani, article cited, p. 34. The date of Babajan's taking up residence at Char Bavadi escaped reporting, and "was possibly by 1910" (Shepherd, *A Sufi Matriarch*, p. 47).

(36) *A Sufi Matriarch* (1986), pp. 51–2. The descriptions of location vary. Ghani says that the neem tree was located "at a place called Malcolm Tank (Char Bavadi) in Cantonment limits" (1939 article, p. 33). Purdom initially referred to "the neem tree in the Malcolm Tank Road" (*The Perfect Master*, p. 20), but later specified "a neem tree in San Jan Mohammad St" (*The God-Man*, p. 19). Kalchuri refers to "the area called Char Bawdi, meaning Four Wells, on Malcolm Tank Road"

(*Lord Meher Vol. One*, p. 13). Dhake Phalkar refers to the "neem tree in Sachapir Street" (*A Visit to Hazrat Babajan*, online). The present writer mentioned "the Char Bavadi vicinity of the cantonment, located on Malcolm Tank Road as it was then known" (*A Sufi Matriarch*, p. 47). According to the hostile report of Green, "Baba Jan established herself beneath a large neem tree next to Malcolm Tank, alongside the boundary wall of the cantonment" (*Islam and the Army in Colonial India*, 2009, p. 129).

(37) Shepherd, *A Sufi Matriarch*, p. 54. The gold bangles were gifted by a wealthy devotee from Bombay. "An unknown thief snatched away these bangles with such lack of grace that one of her wrists was badly lacerated and bled profusely." When a policeman arrived on the scene, Babajan asked him to arrest those who wanted to catch the thief and administer punishment

(38) A basic theme applying to Babajan is here appropriate. "She was persecuted by orthodox religionists but gained an inter-religious following" (Aftab, *Inscribing South Asian Muslim Women*, p. 112, and commenting on *A Sufi Matriarch*).

(39) Ghani, "Hazrat Babajan of Poona" (1939), p. 33.

(40) Shepherd, *A Sufi Matriarch*, p. 53.

(41) Ibid. p. 54. The episode of the stolen shawl was earlier related by Ghani and also featured in Adriel, *Avatar* (1947), p. 40. Adriel refers to Babajan as "God-woman," in a brief account found in a book about Meher Baba. Adriel adopted the "perfect master" theme favoured by Meher Baba. She makes only one reference to Sufism.

(42) Shepherd, *Minds and Sociocultures Vol. One* (1995), pp. 140–1. Cf. Green, *Islam and the Army in Colonial India* (2009), pp. 128ff., for a markedly unsympathetic account of Babajan. I might be allowed an opinion here, as Professor Green cites

my own book exclusively to the effect that the Char Bavadi locale was initially a notorious haunt of toddy drinkers and smokers of opium and cannabis (cf. *A Sufi Matriarch*, pp. 47–8). He fails to duly mention the accompanying details, which attest that the haunt became upgraded as a consequence of Babajan's presence. The haunt actually disappeared after a few years, and with the assistance of Pathan *sepoys*. Green prefers to say "given the location of her den," and comments that such "dens" were a typical feature of every Indian cantonment. The commentator does not supply relevant details of the Poona situation, and instead insinuates that Babajan participated in activities of the den. He even indulges in an unrelated reference to Seroor cantonment, associated in the nineteenth century with "a house of ill repute" at which soldiers liked to assemble. This attempt to implicate or stigmatise Pathans is not commendable. Green flippantly refers to "the low company she [Babajan] kept," which in the context of his demeaning "den" suggestions, represents an acute distortion of events. The treatment is overall one of the most misleading I have seen in academic literature relating to Sufism. The tendency of Professor Green to degrade Babajan (and Pathan *sepoys*) may be seen as symptomatic of more general attitudes, found among the Western academic caste, that relegate or distort the role of citizens. It is relevant to inform here that Babajan was not part of the "den", contrary to the postcolonial elitist imputation. The influential academic caricature of Babajan (published by Cambridge University Press) may indicate an unfortunate trend of misinformation in relation to Islamic minorities. See also note 56 below and Appendice Two.

(43) Purdom says "she was seen in Bombay in 1900, where she stayed for some years, her favourite place of resort being the locality near Pydhowni" (*The Perfect Master*, p. 19). Purdom names both of the male saints. According to Kalchuri, Babajan was seen in Bombay "around 1901," and the two male saints "became part of her circle of disciples" (*Lord Meher Vol. One*, p.

11). According to the same late version, Babajan subsequently imparted "God-Realization to both of them," which remains a very obscure event. Another version of the Bombay phase affirms that Babajan associated herself with *faqir* groupings that comprised a notable subculture in colonial Bombay, especially that led by Abdul Rahman of Dongri (Green, *Islam and the Army in Colonial India*, p. 128). Abdul Rahman of Dongri has been variously described. According to one report, he took strong objection to the occasion when a devotee hung some pictures of Muslim saints in his home at Bandra. Those saints included Sai Baba of Shirdi, Tajuddin Baba of Nagpur, Maulana Saheb, and Abdul Rahman himself. He demanded that these pictures be taken down and thrown into the sea (Warren, *Unravelling the Enigma*, p. 123). This resistance to "image worship" fits an Islamic theme, although extra dimensions may have been in occurrence.

(44) An early notice on Tajuddin Baba appeared in Purdom, *The Perfect Master*, pp. 24–5. A recent, and very conservative, version is Green, *Islam and the Army in Colonial India* (2009), pp. 120–8, who asserts that "the causes and character of Taj al-din's madness remain obscure, as perhaps they were even to himself." The obscurity is not universal. See also E. Bharadwaja, *Shri Tajuddin Baba* (Ongole, n.d.). Other versions have appeared in the Meher Baba literature, including the account by Ghani, "Hazrat Baba Tajuddin of Nagpur" (1939). An early coverage of mine was included in *The Life of Meher Baba* (unpublished manuscript). In *A Sufi Matriarch* (note 41), I referred to a related treatment intended for my unpublished *Survey of the Sufi Phenomenon*.

(45) *A Sufi Matriarch*, p. 59, and suggesting that Babajan's reference to Tajuddin Baba as *faqir* means a "poor one" in the sense of eradicating the limiting *nafs*, a Sufi term denoting personality or ego limitations which obstruct perception and deeper experience. However, in general colonial and postcolonial vocabularies, the word *faqir* was and is simplified

to a negative connotation reflecting the preference of status elites. See further chapter 28 of the present work.

(46) Some scholarly assessments of Abdul Qadir Jilani are very critical of the process in which popular hindsight elevates contradictory features. "Only in 521/1127 when he was over fifty years old did he suddenly come into prominence as a popular preacher in Baghdad. From that date his reputation grew, but as a Hanbali preacher, not as a Sufi. He dressed like an *alim*, not like a Sufi" (Trimingham, *The Sufi Orders in Islam*, p. 42). The *alim* was a religious scholar, one of the *ulama*, a contingent whose attitude to Sufis was often hostile or modifying. Cf. Schimmel, *Mystical Dimensions of Islam* (1975), p. 247, who says that the name of Jilani is "surrounded by innumerable legends that scarcely fit the image of the stern, sober representative of contrition and mystical fear.... a number of sayings are attributed to him in which he claims the highest mystical rank possible."

(47) Shepherd, *A Sufi Matriarch*, pp. 59–60. See also Ghani's supplement to his article "Hazrat Babajan of Poona," reproduced in Kantak, ed., *Hazrat Babajan* (1981), pp. 48–50. Ghani indicates that other mendicants were also in the queue for money gifts from Babajan. He may have personally witnessed this episode. Ghani certainly describes the piercing cold in the early winter morning, and states that "Babajan, being in playful mood indulged in a very humorous spree."

(48) See further Shepherd, *From Oppression to Freedom: A Study of the Kaivani Gnostics* (1988), part one, and containing some cues from Sheriar Irani's son Adi S. Irani, domiciled in London and whom I personally encountered. See also *Sheriar Mundegar Irani and Zoroastrianism* (online article). Sheriar was mentioned anonymously on page 48 of *A Sufi Matriarch* (1986).

(49) Shepherd, *Meher Baba, an Iranian Liberal* (1988), p. 17. See also Shepherd, *Investigating the Sai Baba Movement* (2005), part

three. I hold an unpublished multi-volume work entitled *The Life of Meher Baba*, composed in my early years. See also *Meher Baba and Paul Brunton* (online article).

(50) Kalchuri, *Lord Meher Vol. One*, pp. 196ff. Kalchuri's style (translated from Hindi) has a tendency to be poetic, but he does provide much information. The photographic complement is occasionally erratic. The photo on page 199 is mistakenly described as being taken "after he [Meher Baba] was God-realized by Babajan." In the 1960s, the same photograph was identified by Meher Baba's brothers Jal and Beheram Irani as dating to 1913, meaning before the "God-realization." I know this because I purchased a copy of the photograph at that time from Jal S. Irani.

(51) Purdom, *The Perfect Master*, p. 21. Translations of Babajan's words have varied. The version of Purdom is early.

(52) Shepherd, *Meher Baba, an Iranian Liberal* (1988), p. 17.

(53) Shepherd, *A Sufi Matriarch*, p. 51. Of the pre-1914 period, Kalchuri says: "The religious orthodox or people of high status would seldom approach Babajan because the Pathan soldiers who guarded her were forbidding personages, and the idle beggars who iived off the *dakshina* or money given her by devotees were despicable" (*Lord Meher Vol. One* p. 196).

(54) Charles Purdom reported: "I have met people who in their childhood used to throw stones at her, thinking her to be mad" (*The God-Man*, p. 19).

(55) *A Sufi Matriarch* (1986) p. 65, and citing from the report of Meher Baba found in D. E. Stevens, ed., *Listen Humanity* (1957), pp. 64–5, which informs that "among those who were deeply devoted to her was a large number of Pathan and Baluchi soldiers who would often flock around her seat [place] under the tree." Meher Baba used the Persian word *jalal* to describe the saintly mood of anger or grandeur, a word evocative of a "divine majesty."

(56) See Nile Green, *Islam and the Army in Colonial India* (2009), pp. 128ff, and referring to the "quotidian pleasures of tea-drinking and *ganja*-smoking" amongst the soldiers who gathered around Babajan (ibid., p. 139). That is a misleading statement, and lacks evidence. She herself favoured tea, which she drank frequently. Professor Green gives a brief and unsympathetic portrayal of Babajan, although citing Charles Purdom and Dr. Ghani, and observing that "those accounts, which generally overlap closely, are expanded in K. R. D. Shepherd, *A Sufi Matriarch*" (ibid., p. 186 note 148). Green differs from those accounts in his distorting and conflatory tendency. "While we have no evidence for Babajan's own drug use, each of the accounts of her describes her as no less deranged than Bane Miyan" (ibid., p. 130). The latter part of this statement is not only erroneous, but also extremely offensive. Green is here obsessed with the eccentric image of Bane Miyan (d. 1921), a male *faqir* of distant Aurangabad whose activities were recorded in a very extravagant hagiography entitled *Azam al-Karamat or World of Miracles* (ibid., pp. 90ff.). Further, Green is unable to distinguish Babajan from "tramps" and also "revelling soldiers." The relevant quotation is: "She would have fitted in well in Char Bavadi with the tramps who dropped out there and the revelling soldiers who dropped in for the pleasures of a pipe or a cup of tea" (ibid., p. 130). This very superficial judgment is delivered with no evidence whatever, and amounts to a fantasy more objectionable than many miracle stories. The casual theme is equivalent to: because some *sepoys* in India smoked *ganja*, therefore the Pathan *sepoys* at the *neem* tree were all *ganja* smokers, and therefore Babajan was a patron of *ganja*-smoking. This hazardous logic is no guide to history. In more general terms, there is no advance here upon the biased worldview of Christian missionaries, who viewed Muslim ascetics as an inferior rival; British cantonment officials could also be disapproving of *faqirs* as aliens to Raj politics. Another bias was demonstrated by *jihad* partisans, who urged their children to throw stones at Babajan because of heretical

utterances. Those utterances of Babajan are described by Green as "raving declarations" (ibid., p. 130), even though no verbatim report of them exists. In his postcolonial elitist disparagement, Professor Green even goes to the extent of describing Babajan as "revelling in her filthy degradation of the flesh" (ibid., p. 131). No reference is made to a contrasting interpretation. On the issue of ablutions, see note 34 above.

(57) *Mehera*, ed. J. Judson (1989), pp. 44–5. Mehera subsequently resided at the Meherabad ashram of Meher Baba, and Daulatmai later stayed with Freni at Nasik, maintaining silence for over twenty years at the unusual instruction of Meher Baba. Daulatmai died still silent in 1952.

(58) Babajan liked to wear metal rings. The missing finger was a consequence of this habit. "On account of an ill-fitting ring she lost a finger from her left hand; even when the finger became septic she would not have the ring removed, and sacrificed her finger" (Purdom, *The Perfect Master*, p. 21). Dhake says that the finger was lost from the right hand. See also Shepherd, *A Sufi Matriarch*, pp. 67–8.

(59) M. R. Dhake Phalkar, *A Visit to Hazrat Babajan* (online). This item comes from Dhake's book *In the Company of Meher Baba* (1988), pp. 45–6. At Meherabad during that same decade, Dhake was principal of the institution known as the Hazrat Babajan School, an educational centre named after the Pathan saint, though not otherwise promoting her career in any way. Dhake was not a devotee of Babajan, but well disposed towards her. His account includes the feature of an unusual act of service, i.e. massaging Babajan's legs from knee to ankle, for about fifteen minutes. She allowed the two visitors to do this. When she asked the reason, they explained that Meher Baba had requested them to perform this action.

(60) *A Sufi Matriarch*, p. 47. Useful documentation on the Raj includes C. A. Bayly, *The New Cambridge History of India: Indian Society and the Making of the British Empire* (Cambridge

University Press, 1988); Penderel Moon, *The British Conquest and Domination of India* (2 vols, 1989); Lawrence James, The *Rise and Fall of the British Empire* (1994); James, *Raj: The Making and Unmaking of British India* (1997).

(61) Percival Spear, *A History of India Vol. 2*, p. 146.

(62) Louis Fischer, *The Life of Mahatma Gandhi* (1951), p. 234. Fischer mentions 25 Gurkhas and 25 Baluchis as the riflemen. In other sources, the Baluchis are identified in terms of 25 Pathans and Baluch of 54th Sikhs and 59th Sind Rifles. Some of the riflemen at first shot high into the air, but were reprimanded by Dyer for this act of consideration.

(63) Shepherd, *A Sufi Matriarch*, p. 57. Ghani says of the initial British reaction that "had it been possible they [the Cantonment Board] would unhesitatingly have had Babajan shifted to some out of the way spot" (Ghani 1939, p. 34).

(64) *A Sufi Matriarch*, p. 58. Both Purdom and Ghani have versions of this event. Purdom says that "the Cantonment Board, until it was Indianized, did not welcome Babajan's presence" (*The Perfect Master*, p. 20).

(65) This episode was recounted by Ghani in the "miracles" supplement to his biography of Babajan, and likewise originally published in *The Meher Baba Journal*. It was reprinted in Kantak, ed., *Hazrat Babajan* (1981), pp. 54–5. The date is wrongly given as 1921.

(66) Ghani, "Hazrat Babajan of Poona," 1939, pp. 35–6 (*Awakener* reprint, p. 17; 1981 reprint, p. 29). See also Shepherd, *A Sufi Matriarch*, pp. 61–2.

(67) This anecdote is included in Ghani's supplement to his biography, known as *Miracles of Babajan*. Ghani maintained an interest in cures, having been a homeopathic doctor after attending Poona Medical School. He clearly did believe that Babajan's cures were effective, and had witnessed some of these personally.

(68) Shepherd, *A Sufi Matriarch*, pp. 67–8, and observing that Babajan "had an aversion to artificial methods and applications, and appears to have regarded European medicine with the same circumspection as she did the hemp and opium of the local drug addicts." Ghani specifies the different metals of the favoured rings in his supplement. In addition, a silver ring was mentioned by Dhake Phalkar.

(69) Kalchuri, *Lord Meher Vol. One*, pp. 17–18, informing that Babajan was averse to gifts of jewellery, but would never remove the cheap rings on her fingers. The precise reason for this preference is not known.

(70) Babajan's linguistic recourse in Poona seems to have been Urdu more than any other language. The prevalent Indian language in the cantonment area has since been Hindi. Professor Anne Feldhaus, a Marathi-speaking expert on Poona (Pune), has reported on the Internet: "Many more Indians in Pune are Muslims, and many of them are more comfortable using Hindi or Urdu than Marathi." See also A. Feldhaus, ed., *Images of Women in Maharashtrian Society* (1998).

(71) Shepherd, *A Sufi Matriarch*, pp. 65–6, and citing Ghani, whose biography includes explanations by Meher Baba about cryptic expressions of Babajan (1939 article, pp. 36–7). According to Meher Baba, the reference to "vermin" signifies a process of destroying crude impressions (of actions) incoming from the outside world, which "perfect saints like Babajan" convert into spiritualised *amal* or "actions," and in a greater quantity than the crude "actions" destroyed (or purified). Cf. Kalchuri, *Lord Meher Vol. One*, endnote to page 17, which has another version of Meher Baba's explanation. Instead of the *amal* theme, Hindu terminology is employed (i.e. *sanskaras*); however, the meaning is much the same.

(72) Purdom, *The Perfect Master*, p. 107, reports this development, and also how Meher Baba interpreted these events in terms of meaning that Babajan was nearing the time of her death.

(73) *A Sufi Matriarch*, pp. 68–9. I gleaned this information during the 1960s, as a consequence of familiarity with the Meher Baba literature, which is the major source for Babajan. The Muslim devotees of Babajan had oral traditions, but these were not written down, in contrast to the accounts of Ghani, Purdom, and others.

(74) Kalchuri, *Lord Meher Vol. 3* (1988), pp. 1036–7. The Meherabad event was described many years earlier by Abdul Kareem (Ramju) Abdulla, a Muslim member of the *mandali* who wrote a book about the Meher/Prem Ashram of that period shortly after the events described. See Deitrick, ed., *Ramjoo's Diaries 1922-1929*, pp. 464ff. Ramju emphasises that many persons at Meherabad were amazed that Babajan had come there, so unprecedented was the event. Kalchuri (who was not present) says the *mandali* bowed at Babajan's feet; such an action would have contravened her general ruling. Ramju does not have this detail, and says instead that Meher Baba "ordered all the boys and disciples to pay their long due respects and love to his own master." The original was in Ramju Abdulla, *Sobs and Throbs, or Some Spiritual Sidelights* (1929), p. 89. Ramju reported Meher Baba's words as: "This is the most eventful day of my career." Moreover, there are also differences found in another account from Esphandiar Vesali, an Irani Zoroastrian who was part of the Meher/ Prem Ashram and a direct witness of the Babajan event (*Ramjoo's Diaries*, p. 522). Vesali says that everyone greeted Babajan, beginning with the men and afterwards the Prem Ashram boys (including Vesali). This source informs that Babajan was more intimate with the boys than with the men, and "would take our faces and put our cheeks next to hers and then after a while she would let go" (ibid.). Ramju does not mention this intimacy as occurring on the first visit, but does refer to a similar event in relation to Babajan's second visit to Meherabad. The Vesali interview was recorded in Iran during 1975. Meher Baba's brother Adi S. Irani (whom I met in London) had a version of related events, which

were covered in my unpublished *Life of Meher Baba*. See also Shepherd, *Meher Baba, an Iranian Liberal*, pp. 254–5, on the Ramju Abdulla materials.

(75) Deitrick, ed., *Ramjoo's Diaries,* p. 468; Kalchuri (1988), p. 1047. Kalchuri says that the cars crossed on both journeys to and fro, but neither vehicle stopped. He relates that Babajan embraced the adult male devotees (the *mandali*) and kissed each of the Prem ashram boys. Ramju refers to "pats and caresses." These boys had been undergoing their own "spiritual adventures" recently; Babajan appears to have felt a strong affinity with them. The Prem ashram included Muslim, Hindu, and Zoroastrian inmates.

(76) Paul Brunton, *A Search In Secret India* (London: Rider, no date, but published 1934), p. 64.

(77) Shepherd, *Meher Baba, an Iranian Liberal*, p. 148, in an account relaying various other events neglected by Brunton (alias H. Raphael Hirsch).

(78) Brunton, *op. cit.*, p. 62. According to Brunton, devotees of Meher Baba claimed that Babajan was 130 years old. Purdom reported that the date of birth was "supposed to have been about 1790" on the basis of Indian informants, although astutely observing that the actual date was unknown (*The Perfect Master*, p. 19). Ghani opted for 125 years life duration.

(79) On Upasni Maharaj, see part two of Shepherd, *Investigating the Sai Baba Movement* (2005).

(80) *A Search in Secret India*, p. 64. This reflection also appeared in the caption to a photograph of Babajan that was employed by Brunton's publisher. The same photograph also appeared in the British newspaper *Daily Sketch* in April 1932, reporting that Babajan was said to be 130 years old at the time of her death. There are two well-known photos of her, one of these retouched by Meelan Photo Studio, Poona, in the 1960s, as I

learned when I purchased a copy of this portrait in 1966 (and see *Investigating the Sai Baba Movement,* p. 302).

(81) See Jeffrey Masson, *My Father's Guru* (1994); Shepherd, *Meher Baba, an Iranian Liberal*, pp. 146–76; Shepherd, *Meher Baba and Paul Brunton* (online article); Stephen J. Castro, *Critics of Meher Baba* (online).

(82) Malcolm Schloss, "Thus Have I Heard" (1966), pp. 3–4. Schloss was an American devotee of Meher Baba, and stayed near the latter in India during 1936–7, where he learned of various past episodes from the *mandali*. The meeting with Babajan lacks a close date, but the informant (Adi S. Irani) specified the summer months of 1931. The details were known only to relatively few of Meher Baba's devotees, and surfaced thirty-five years later in the version of Schloss. The information was included in my unpublished *Life of Meher Baba*, vol. one, p. 484 ms. A complexity in the preliminaries to this meeting was that Babajan sent repeated messages to Meher Baba, to the effect that she wanted to meet him. Yet he consistently refused.

(83) Ghani, "Miracles of Babajan" (repr. Kantak, ed., *Hazrat Babajan*, 1981, p. 56).

(84) Ghani, "Hazrat Babajan of Poona" (1939), p. 38. Babajan's tomb (*dargah*) is small by comparison with some others. The adjoining road has become increasingly busy. With regard to her uncertain age, all estimates are provisional. In *A Sufi Matriarch*, pp. 77–8 note 54, I concluded that "there seems every ground to believe that the subject was over a hundred by the time of her death." I also commented: "In view of the repeated assertions as to Babajan's great age, I think it possible that she may have been born c. 1820 or even earlier" (ibid., p. 72 note 16).

(85) J. Spencer Trimingham. *The Sufi Orders in Islam* (1971), p. 176.

(86) Shepherd, *A Sufi Matriarch*, p. 22, and also referring to the figure of Jahanara, daughter of the Mughal emperor Shah Jahan. "Though formally initiated into the Qadiri order of dervishes, there was no question of her [Jahanara's] formal recognition as a member of any dervish hierarchy" (ibid.).

(87) Ghani, "Hazrat Babajan of Poona" (1939), p. 30. This suggestion was accompanied by the interpretation of a *qalandar* legend concerning "three Qalandars on earth signifying the end of the world." The exegesis sounds far-fetched to some analysts, and is less successful than the biographical details supplied by the same writer.

(88) Ghani, article cited, p. 38. Ghani enthusiastically asserted that Babajan was "the second manifestation of Divinity on earth, in the female form, after the famous Rabia of Basrah" (p. 29). His argument about the "Qalandari Era" attaches to a tradition he associated with the "Qalandariyah order," which he mentions in relation to an "utter disregard of external law (Shariat) and for the utterance of gnosis, shocking to orthodoxy." Ghani mentions a parable featuring the name of Bu Ali (Shah) Qalandar, but no history is forthcoming. Cf. Bruce B. Lawrence, *Notes from a Distant Flute: Sufi Literature in Pre-Mughal India* (1978), p. 79, describing Bu Ali Shah Qalandar (d. 1324) in terms of: "Though frequently linked to the Chishti *silsilah* [lineage], he seems to have had no formal attachment to a *pir*; like other *qalandars*, he belonged to the Uwaysi tradition. Some of his alleged works, such as *Hukmnamah* and *Hikmatnama*, are almost certainly spurious." Cf. Rizvi, *A History of Sufism in India Vol. One* (1978), p. 305, who says: "Whatever his spiritual lineage, Sheikh Abu Ali Qalandar was a scholar and a stern ascetic who renounced the world and became totally engrossed in self-mortification and contemplation. As a *qalandar* he refused to observe the rules of the *Sharia* [religious law]. Nevertheless he approved when Maulana Ziya ud-Din Sunnami, an orthodox *alim* [religious scholar], clipped his moustache to the length required by holy

law." Bu Ali Shah lived at Panipat in the Punjab, to where
his father had emigrated from Iraq.

(89) Annemarie Schimmel, *The Triumphal Sun: A Study of
the Works of Jalaloddin Rumi* (1993), pp. 18ff., and adding
that "there are utterances by Shams which fit well into this
[*qalandar*] picture, and Rumi's later praise of the *qalandar*
seems to point to the same fact" (ibid., p. 20).

(90) A. J. Arberry, *Discourses of Rumi* (1961), p. 6, referring to
Shams in terms of "A native of Tabriz seemingly of artisan
origin, suddenly arrived in the Saljuq capital and attracted
attention by the wildness of his demeanour."

(91) S. A. A. Rizvi, *A History of Sufism in India Vol. One*,
p. 303, and referring to the related Qalandariyya and
Jawaliqi traditions. Chishti writings did not distinguish
between these groupings. The same scholar informs that
the Mongol conquest of Central Asia and Iran facilitated the
movement of Qalandar and Jawaliqi groups from Turkey
and Egypt to India. Passing through Multan in the Punjab,
these mendicants frequently came into friction with Shaikh
Bahauddin Zakariyya (1182–1262), who "disliked *qalandars*
intensely" (ibid., p. 306). Born near Multan, Zakariyya was
a famous and wealthy *shaikh* of the Suhrawardi order. In
Baghdad, he had become the *khalifa* (deputy) of Shihabuddin
Suhrawardi (d. 1234), author of the *Awarif al-Maarif.* Back
in Multan, Zakariyya clashed with the local *ulama*, and
established a large *khanaqah* complete with granaries. This
centre was not open to the common people. "Only eminent
religious people, and perhaps state dignitaries and wealthy
merchants, were admitted" (ibid., p. 191). The mood of upper
class ambience and closeted theological discussion were
evidently factors in dispute with the mendicant *qalandars*.

(92) Trimingham, *The Sufi Orders in Islam*, p. 267. In the
relevant passage, Shihabuddin Suhrawardi (d. 1234) stated
that the word *qalandariyya* was applied to those mystics who

"respect no custom or usage and reject the regular observances of society.... they concern themselves little with ritual prayer and fasting" (ibid.). Cf. J.T.P. De Bruijn, "The *Qalandariyyat* in Mystical Poetry, from Sanai Onwards" (1992), p. 76, who says: "There is no indication that Suhrawardi meant by this [i.e. destruction of conventions] anything else but a tendency which began to manifest itself in the life of the Sufis in his age." The same scholar refers to the legend that a group known as "followers of the *qalandar* way" emerged about 1223 in Damascus, from where they spread to Egypt and other countries. The founder was reputedly Sayed Jamaluddin from Sawa in Iran, who introduced basic *qalandar* habits, e.g. the complete shaving of hair on the head, the wearing of sackcloth, and a mendicant career. Marginalised dervish groupings are an obscure feature of Sufism. See further Karamustafa, *God's Unruly Friends: Dervish Groups in the Islamic Later Middle Period, 1200-1550* (1994).

(93) Rizvi, *A History of Sufism in India Vol. One*, pp. 307–9. Sidi Maula was an immigrant who settled at Delhi and became involved in politics, ignoring the contrary advice of the Chishti saint Baba Farid (d. 1265). A wealthy man, Sidi Maula maintained a *khanaqah* attracting noblemen and military generals. He ended up in chains, having become implicated in a plot to assassinate the Sultan. His tragic fate served as a confirmation of the Chishti principle: never dabble in political events. On the Chishtis, see Carl Ernst, *Eternal Garden* (1992); Muneera Haeri, *The Chishtis: A Living Light* (2000); Ernst and Lawrence, *Sufi Martyrs of Love* (2002).

(94) *A History of Sufism in India Vol. One*, pp. 306. Nimati *qalandars* were very active in India during the Mughal era. The Nimatullahi order exercised a strong influence in Iran, but also suffered enduring harassment from Shi'ite clericalism. See further P. L. Wilson and N. Pourjavardy, *Kings of Love: The Poetry and History of the Ni'matullahi Sufi Order* (1976); Javad Nurbakhsh, *Masters of the Path: A History of the Nimatullahi Sufi Order* (1980).

(95) The mediator for Ibn al-Arabi was Sadruddin Qunawi (d. 1274), who supplied a systematised format and also coined the name *wahdat al-wujud* (Oneness of Being). "This expression has the definite merit of offering a simple and handy designation for Ibn Arabi's doctrine; but it is also highly reductive, and provided Ibn Arabi's critics with a dangerous weapon." Quotation from Claude Addas, *Quest for the Red Sulphur: The Life of Ibn Arabi* (1993), p. 232.

(96) Jamal J. Elias, *The Throne Carrier of God: The Life and Thought of Ala ad-dawla as-Simnani* (1995), pp. 57–8, 97ff., referring to Simnani's "deep-rooted opposition to any doctrine which compromised divine unity and transcendence.... for Simnani there is no possibility of union with the divine, and individuals such as Bistami, Hallaj and Ibn al-Arabi are accomplished mystics who, unfortunately, have... fallen into the trap of self-delusion" (ibid., pp. 97–8). Professor Rizvi described Simnani as "a vehement exponent of the *wahdat al-shuhud*" (*A Hist of Sufism in India Vol. Two*, p. 190). According to Professor Elias, "Simnani's influence on [Shaikh Ahmad] Sirhindi must be greater than is usually assumed" (Elias, *op. cit.*, p. 162).

(97) M. Mujeeb, *The Indian Muslims* (1967), p. 303. Abdul Quddus Gangohi was a Sabiri Chishti and prolific writer. His tendencies were orthodox, although he did pen the *Rushd-Nama*, a treatise "which implicitly adapts Hindu practices to the discipline of Sufism" (Lawrence, *Notes from a Distant Flute*, p. 58). This treatise includes his own verses and those of his teachers, and these verses "identify sufi beliefs based on the *Wahdat al-Wujud* with the philosophy and practices of Gorakhnath," the legendary Nath Yogi (Rizvi. *Hist. of Sufism in India Vol. One*, p. 336). Despite that poetic tendency to liberalism, the social and political attitude of Gangohi was severely orthodox, as evidenced in a letter to the emperor Babur. Gangohi here urged that no *kafir* (infidel non-Muslim) should be elected to any administrative position, that *kafirs* should be forced to pay regular taxes, that their garb should

differ from Muslims, and that their worship should be conducted in secret (ibid., p. 345-6). This attitude amounted to a defence of upper-class Muslims. On Gangohi, see also Shepherd, *Some Philosophical Critiques and Appraisals* (2004), pp. 148–50, and relaying: "His family were *ulama* with Sufi affiliations. He apparently believed that he was a *qutub*, which is a very exalted rank in Sufi hierarchical thinking. Though he urged the necessity of strict religious orthodoxy, he [Gangohi] held several views which actually conflicted with the consensus of Sunni belief, including his advocacy of Ibn al-Arabi's monistic doctrine of *wahdat al-wujud*" (ibid., p. 149).

(98) M. Mujeeb, *The Indian Muslims*, p. 304. Although Shaikh Husain seemed so non-communicative, it is evident that he had a very subtle mind and adopted a particular strategy in his audiences. According to Mujeeb, this entity was "a remarkable person." If pressed to talk, Husain spoke of trivial things. For instance, when Gangohi visited him, Husain asked if it was true that red melons could be cultivated at the former's hometown of Rudauli. The exasperated Gangohi tried to pin his host down to explaining a verse fraught with religious significations. Husain then turned to the gathering, and said politely that questions like this only occurred to Gangohi because he had adopted the life of an ascetic and was wearing the robe of a Sufi. Husain then identified the verse as being composed by the heretical Sufi Ain al-Quzat Hamadani, who had been executed a few centuries before. Husain observed that Hamadani "has written that one of two interpretations can be put on everything he says: that it is true, and that it is false" (ibid.). Meaning true to Sufis like Junayd and Shibli, and false to the externalist *ulama*. Husain continued: "If now you want the interpretation of the externalist *ulama*, I would say I am not a scholar." He carefully added that "I am not a Junaid or a Shibli" (ibid.). In this manner, Husain adroitly parried the pointed question. It is deducible that the factor of wearing a Sufi robe did not

inspire this *qalandar* with any confidence. The Sufi robe had become an apparatus of religious scholars, who might easily arrive at a censorious conclusion best avoided.

(99) Shepherd, *From Oppression to Freedom* (1988), pp. 118ff., informing that Muhammad Sa'id Sarmad was an Armenian Jew, the descendant of a family of rabbis, who spent his earlier years at Kashan and Shiraz. Sarmad had strong affinities with both *ishraq* (illuminism) and *wahdat al-wujud,* the former taught by ishraqi Suhrawardi (d. 1191), not to be confused with Suhrawardi of Baghdad who authored the *Awarif al-Maarif.*

(100) Rizvi, *A Hist. of Sufism in India Vol. One,* p. 403. Rizvi emphasises that, in Indian Sufism, women continued to play a role as Sufis and as the mothers of leading Sufis. Shaikh Abdul Haqq Muhaddith Dehlawi (d. 1642) wrote a separate chapter on Indian Muslim women saints in his celebrated *Akhbar al-Akhyar* (ibid., p. 401). A Qadiri Sufi and scholar of prophetic traditions, Abdul Haqq applied his skill to over two hundred biographies of Indian Sufis. "He scrupulously excluded all references to supernatural and miraculous elements, highlighting instead the mystical and spiritual ideas, ethical behaviour and psychological perceptions" of his subjects (ibid., p. 12). Another scholar says that Abdul Haqq "brought together the extravagances of the *sufis,* the meticulousness of the righteous *ulama* and the ideal of orthodoxy" (Mujeeb, *The Indian Muslims,* p. 276). A Western scholar describes the *Akhbar al-Akhyar* as depicting over 260 Sufis from the Chishti, Suhrawardi, Firdawsi, Shattari, and Qadiri orders, along with the Qalandariyya. "A short appendix includes fourteen pious women." See Lawrence, "An Indo-Persian Perspective on the Significance of Early Persian Sufi Masters" (1993), p. 23.

(101) Margaret Smith, *Rabi'a the mystic and her fellow-saints in Islam* (1928), pp. 1–3. 137, and citing the French scholar

Louis Massignon on Rabia as the "saint par excellence of the Sunnite hagiography."

(102) A. J. Arberry, trans., *Muslim Saints and Mystics: Episodes from the Tadhkirat al-Auliya* (1966), p. 39.

(103) Ahmet T. Karamustafa, *Sufism: The Formative Period* (2007), p. 3, and informing that the earliest writer to mention Rabia was the *litterateur* al-Jahiz (d. 868/9), who gave no biographical details and referred to her as being one of the ascetics of Basra. A century followed before she appeared in the works of Sufi writers like Sulami. There was some degree of confusion with her contemporary Rabia bint Ismail of Syria.

(104) See Rkia E. Cornell, ed. and trans., *Early Women Sufis: Dhikr an-niswa al-muta'abbidat as-sufiyyat* (1999).

(105) Margaret Smith, *Rabia the Mystic*, pp. 111ff., especially p. 126. Reference to this point was made in Shepherd, *The Resurrection of Philosophy* (1989), p. 149, and commenting: "Much sufi history is a record of friction with dogmatists, though there were also many dogmatists who became popular as sufis, usually as a result of their conviction that they had achieved the merits of this fabled category."

(106) R. A. Nicholson, trans., *Kashf al-Mahjub of Al Hujwiri: The Oldest Persian Treatise on Sufism* (1936), p. 358. The *Kashf* was apparently partly written in Lahore, a city in the Punjab. "It is probable that oral tradition was the main source from which al-Hujwiri derived the materials for his work" (ibid., p. xv). According to Nicholson, the objective was "to set forth a complete system of Sufism" (ibid., p. xii). What we find here is orthodox Sufism.

(107) Claude Addas, *Quest for the Red Sulphur: The Life of Ibn Arabi* (1993), p. 87. The mother of Ibn al-Arabi was also a visitor to Fatima, a factor suggesting "an orientation on her

part towards Sufism" (ibid., p. 25). Another female teacher of Arabi was Shams Umm al-Faqara, whom he encountered *circa* 1190. "She concealed her spiritual state, but sometimes she would reveal an aspect of it to me in secret" (ibid., p. 88).

(108) Annemarie Schimmel, *Mystical Dimensions of Islam* (1975), p. 432.

(109) Ibid., and informing that one of these convents in Egypt was a refuge for divorced women. In more general terms, Schimmel writes that "many religious leaders admitted that they received not only their first religious instruction but also their preliminary training in the mystical path [Sufism] from their mothers" (ibid., p. 430). This factor can be viewed as a counterweight to the monolithic influence of the *ulama* (male religious professors) in Islamic society.

(110) See J. K. Birge, *The Bektashi Order of Dervishes* (1937). The Bektashi founder was reputedly Haji Bektash (d. *circa* 1335), a legendary figure who emigrated from distant Khorasan. See also Schimmel, *Mystical Dimensions of Islam*, pp. 338ff., observing that from the fifteenth century, Bektashi leaders were closely involved with the Janissaries, administering guidance to these soldiers. "Thus they were, logically, involved in the fall of the Janissaries in 1826, when this corps was uprooted because of its increasingly destructive role in Ottoman society" (ibid., p. 339).

(111) Schimmel, *op, cit.*, p. 432. The Turkish scholar Koprulu (zade) suggested that shamanistic elements from the Turko-Mongolian world reappeared under the auspices of certain dervish orders, especially the Yasaviyya and Bektashiyya. In this connection are implicated the inclusion of women in meetings, the performance of *zikr* exercises, and survivals in regalia such as forms of headgear. See M. F. Kopruluzade, *Influence de Chamanisme Turko-Mongol* (1929). The author also dwells on the Rifai order in relation to the Mongol invasion (pp. 12ff.), and depicts Barak Baba of the late thirteenth

century Ilkhanid era as an example of the influence of Mongol shamanism on Sufism (pp. 14ff.).

(112) Schimmel, *Mystical Dimensions of Islam*, pp. 433, 435.

(113) *The Dabistan* (Shea and Troyer trans.) Vol. 3; *The Religion of the Sufis* (London: Octagon Press, 1979), p. 80. The author of the *Dabistan* says that he personally knew Mulla Shah. The *Dabistan-i Mazahib* is a distinctive seventeenth century work of uncertain authorship, having been differently attributed to Muslim and Zoroastrian composers. Nevertheless, affiliation to the Azar Kaivan school is evident.

(114) Bikrama Jit Hasrat, *Dara Shikuh: Life and Works* (1982), pp. 87–8. The details come from Dara Shikoh's work *Sakinat al-Awliya*, a biographical work on saints of the Qadiri order in India. Another well-known work of the prince is *Safinat al-Awliya*, a more wide-ranging compendium in which over 400 biographical entries figure, ending with a section on female saints. Shikoh acknowledges here his debt to similar works, especially Jami's *Nafahat al-Uns*. He emphasises his membership of the Qadiri order, and styles himself as "the servant of the saints, Dara Shikuh *Hanafi, Qadiri*, son of Shah Jahan" (ibid., pp. 43ff.). Cf. Lawrence, "An Indo-Persian Perspective" (1993), pp. 24–5, stating that *Safinat al-Awliya* contains "fragmentary biographical resumes of some four hundred saints, both Indian and non-Indian; preceding these accounts are other biographies of Muslim notables, beginning with the Prophet Muhammad." Though "fascinated by the miraculous," Shikoh also evidences a concern with historical accuracy. This is nevertheless seen by Professor Lawrence as "a mask for his overriding goal: not only to affirm Abd al-Qadir [Jilani] as the foremost Sufi exemplar and the Qadiriyya as the paramount spiritual brotherhood, but to underpin his own authority vis-à-vis rival claims to Qadiri spirituality." Shikoh is here also seen to have modelled many of his entries on longer ones in the *Akhbar al-Akhyar* of his older Qadiri contemporary Abdul-Haqq Muhaddith

Dehlawi (d. 1642). Yet Shikoh bypassed the rival lineage traced by the latter. This indicates an arbitrary factor in such presentations. It should also be taken into account that Dara Shikoh was only 25 years old when he completed the *Safinat al-Awliya* in 1640. According to Rizvi, Shikoh here cultivated "an obsessive belief that the five main Sufi orders in India (the Qadiriyya, Naqshbandiyya, Chishtiyya, Kubrawiyya, and Suhrawardiyya) were the pivot on which all worldly and spiritual matters depended" (*Hist. of Sufism in India Vol. Two*, p. 129). Within this scheme of reference, "he continued to press the superiority of the Qadiriyya" (ibid., p. 134). He relied heavily upon the hagiology attaching to Abdul Qadir Jilani (d. 1166), the Qadiri founder.

(115) Hasrat, *Dara Shikuh*, p. 84. Jahanara at first wondered whether she would benefit from joining the Qadiri order, and reports a "peculiar 'state' — —which was neither sleep nor wakefulness" that granted a vision which reassured her (ibid., p. 85). She wrote an account of Mulla Shah called the *Sahabiya*.

(116) S. A. A. Rizvi, *A History of Sufism in India Vol. Two* (1983), p. 128. The liberalism of Dara Shikoh is beyond question. *Majma al-Bahrain* was composed some sixteen years after his *Safinat al-Awliya* (note 114 above), and can be viewed as a progression. See also Richards, *The Mughal Empire* (1993), pp. 151ff., on the war of succession.

(117) Schimmel, *Islam in the Indian Subcontinent* (Leiden: E. J. Brill, 1980), pp. 98–100; Rizvi, *op. cit.*, pp. 122ff., 480–1, and observing that European contemporaries misunderstood Jahanara's situation of caring for her deposed father; the travellers Bernier and Manucci wrongly accused her of incestuous relations.

(118) M. Lal and J. D. Westbrook, trans., *The Diwan of Zeb-Un-Nissa* (London: John Murray, 1913), introduction by Westbrook, pp. 7–23; Jan Marek, "Persian Literature in India"

(1968) p. 729; A. Schimmel, *Islam in the Indian Subcontinent,* pp. 101–2; Tahera Aftab, *Inscribing South Asian Muslim Women: An Annotated Bibliography and Research Guide* (Leiden: Brill, 2008), pp. 57ff.; Annie Krieger Krynicki, *Captive Princess: Zebunnisa, Daughter of Emperor Aurangzeb* (2006).

(119) Rizvi, *A History of Sufism in India Vol. Two,* p. 490. No date is given for these letters. Rizvi also mentions the letters to Aurangzeb from Shaikh Muhammad Ubaidullah (1628–1672), another grandson of Sirhindi, who composed a tract for the emperor emphasising "the importance of dissociation from infidels" (ibid.). This insular overture was evidently well received. Ubaidullah was invited to the royal palace several times.

(120) On Sirhindi, see Rizvi, *op. cit.,* pp. 196ff. Sirhindi rejected some concepts of Ibn al-Arabi, and his emerging belief in *wahdat al-shuhud* "synchronised with a firm conviction that he had been divinely commissioned to act as the renewer (*mujaddid*) of the second millennium of Islam" (ibid., p. 213). Sirhindi's claims aroused opposition during his lifetime, and he was temporarily imprisoned by the emperor Jehangir. His followers in subsequent generations glorified his activities, and some modern scholars assisted the legendary portrayal (Rizvi, *Muslim Revivalist Movements,* 1965, p. 215).

(121) See Yohanan Friedmann, *Shaykh Ahmad Sirhindi: An Outline of his Thought and a Study of his Image in the Eyes of Posterity* (1971), an analysis disputing hagiological portrayals. Yet despite the excesses of Mujadiddi lore, Dr. Friedmann deduces that Sirhindi did recommend some of the insular measures against non-Muslims that were later implemented by Aurangzeb (ibid., pp. 7ff., 87ff.). Sirhindi believed that the honour of Islam demanded the severe humiliation of Hindus, and wrote in one of his letters that "whenever a Jew is killed, it is for the benefit of Islam." The bigotry is disconcerting. Cf. Mhd Abdul Haq Ansari, *Sufism and Shariah: A Study of*

Shaykh Ahmad Sirhindi's Effort to Reform Sufism (1986). Cf. J. G. J. Ter Haar, *Follower and Heir of the Prophet: Shaykh Ahmad Sirhindi (1564-1624) as Mystic* (1992). Cf. Arthur F. Buehler, *Revealed Grace: The Juristic Sufism of Ahmad Sirhindi* (2011), supplying a translation from the letters (*maktubat*) of Sirhindi. See also Green, *Sufism Since the Seventeenth Century* (2006), pp. 18–19, referring to events in the Deccan, where Aurangabad played a prominent role in discrediting Sirhindi's doctrines. In 1679, the imperial *shaikh al-Islam* composed a decree at the instruction of Aurangzeb, warning the *qazi* (legist) of Aurangabad about the danger posed by Mujaddidis. This measure was apparently not entirely successful, and in 1682 a renewed appeal was made to the *ulama* of the Hejaz.

(122) Shaikh Muhammad Masum (1599–1161/2) was the third son of Ahmad Sirhindi. The partisan sources assert that his early attainment of spiritual states caused his father to describe him as a future *qutub* (the highest rank in the Sufi spiritual hierarchy). Before 1623, Sirhindi made Masum his successor, informing this son that he had been appointed a *qaiyum* (divine agent) by God. In 1623, Masum visited his father at Ajmer, where "the robe of this exalted position [*qaiyum*] was conferred on him" (Rizvi 1983, p. 242). The Mujaddidi lore generated "the claim that no spiritual or worldly event could take place except at the express command of the *Qaiyums*" (ibid., p. 25).

(123) Rizvi, *A Hist. of Indian Sufism Vol. Two*, p. 244, informing: "Naqshbandiyya hagiologies assert that the princes and nobles of Aurangzeb's court obeyed Saifu'd-Din's orders on all religious matters." However, the chronicles of Aurangzeb do not mention this figure after June 1669, when the monarch visited Saifuddin in the residence assigned for the latter's use in Delhi. See also ibid., pp. 482ff.

(124) Rizvi, *A Hist. of Sufism in India Vol. Two*, p. 491, concluding that Aurangzeb's "policies of discrimination against the Hindus and Shi'is were confined to very limited

political and economic spheres, and were designed to implement Sunni orthodoxy" (ibid.). In this interpretation, "Aurangzeb did help the Naqshbandiyyas, but not at the cost of political expediency" (ibid.).

(125) Rizvi, *Muslim Revivalist Movements* (1965) p. 427. See also Rizvi, *Religious and Intellectual History of the Muslims in Akbar's Reign* (1975). The religious insularism that hallmarked the reign of Aurangzeb is reminiscent of the holy war against Tibet in 1532, led by Sultan Said Khan who had assumed "the saintly ways of the khwajas" and who believed that holy war (*jihad*) was one of "surest roads to salvation and union with God." These quotes are from N. Elias and E. Denison Ross, trans., *A History of the Moghuls of Central Asia: The Tarikh-i-Rashidi of Mirza Muhammad Haidar* (second edn., 1898; repr. London, 1972), p. 403.

(126) Rizvi, *Muslim Revivalist Movements*, p. 427. In a foreword to the same work, Professor Muhammad Habib stated that Dr. Rizvi had proved how the agents of Ahmad Sirhindi had failed at Agra and many other places, and that the legends about the Mujaddid faction controlling political affairs were created by writers very ignorant of history. This in reference to popular legends about the Mujaddidi *qaiyums* (agents of God) changing the ideology of the Sunni community, and controlling all political events of their time (ibid., pp. ix–xi). Rizvi also revealed a dichotomy of approach amongst Naqshbandis of the sixteenth century. While some of these men were conservatives preoccupied with the restoration of *shariat* (religious law), others extended active support to the liberal policy of the emperor Akbar (ibid., pp. 181–2). The puritanical trend gained force at the end of Akbar's reign, the exponents including Khwaja Khawand Mahmud Naqshbandi (d. 1642), who campaigned for the complete suppression of Shia Muslims during the reign of Shah Jahan (ibid., pp. 182ff.). Yet the more well-known Muhammad Baqi Billah (d. 1603) was a moderate, shunning publicity and living a secluded life at Lahore and Delhi (he was born

in Kabul). Baqi Billah believed that the criticisms of *wahdat al-wujud* by Simnani were superficial; he instead supported the viewpoint of Ibn al-Arabi, in alignment with *shariat*; this was the favoured perspective of a large number of Indian Sufis (ibid., pp. 185ff.). Sirhindi was a reputed disciple of Baqi Billah, an episode which is glorified in hagiology. Another associate of the latter was Abdul Haqq Muhaddith Dehlawi (d. 1642), who was critical of Sirhindi's argument against the philosophy of Ibn al-Arabi, and who in a letter to Sirhindi, made the accusation: "The pretensions made by you are such as have never been made by anyone else" (ibid., pp. 268–70, 288). Abdul Haqq was a Qadiri and traditionist of repute. He "sharply criticised the Mujaddid's mystical revelations and drew upon his encyclopaedic knowledge to dispute the Mujaddid's writings" (Rizvi, *Hist. of Sufism in India Vol. Two*, p. 6). On Baqi Billah, see also ibid., pp. 185ff. For subsequent developments, see Arthur F. Buehler, *Sufi Heirs of the Prophet* (1998).

(127) Ernst, *Eternal Garden* (1992), pp. 223–5. "His own simple tomb is technically nothing but an uncovered dirt grave" (ibid., p. 224). This site is close to the tomb of Shaikh Zaynuddin Shirazi (d. 1369). Aurangzeb had frequently visited Khuldabad as a pilgrim. This was a major tomb site in the Deccan, in a region renowned for early Chishti activity involving Burhanuddin Gharib and his disciples.

(128) Gijs Kruijtzer, *Xenophobia in Seventeenth Century India* (2009), p. 273. The same letter of Aurangzeb complains that "there is no province or district where the grovelling infidels have not raised a tumult" (ibid.). In the aspersive Mughal parlance, the official name for Marathas was "robbers" (*ashqiya*). On the Deccan wars of Aurangzeb, see further Richards, *The Mughal Empire* (1993), pp. 205ff. See also Gordon, *The Marathas 1600-1818* (1993), esp. pp. 59ff. on Shivaji.

(129) Kruijtzer, *Xenophobia*, pp. 272-3, 275, and informing that "Bahri was sympathetic to the *majzubs,* Sufis unattached to any of the orders." The characteristics of this category vary in reports and definitions. Some remarks on *majzubs* (*majazib*), in relation to the Deccan, are included in Shepherd, *Investigating the Sai Baba Movement* (2005), pp. 47-54, 172-3, and also relevant to some material found in Eaton, *Sufis of Bijapur 1300-1700* (1978). My version of the issue concluded that "the *majazib* were a diffuse phenomenon operating at many levels in eighteenth century Deccani counterculture, which included degenerates" (*Investigating,* p. 47). The *majazib* associated with Bijapur "comprised a trend which opposed the urban and landed Sufis" (ibid.). On the more extensive data relating to this territory, see Eaton, *A Social History of the Deccan 1300-1761* (2005).

(130) Kruijtzer, *Xenophobia,* p. 277. Ahmedabad was situated in Gujarat. Kruijtzer informs that the riot of 1714 was followed by a "near-riot" at the same city in 1716, and in relation to cow-slaughter. In the 1720s, a number of riots occurred between Muslims and Hindus in North India and Kashmir. The worst riots occurred over two centuries later, during the explosive period of partition between Pakistan and India.

Bibliography

Abdulla, Abdul Kareem (Ramju), *Sobs and Throbs, or Some Spiritual Sidelights* (Ahmednagar: N. N. Satha, 1929).

Addas, Claude, *Quest for the Red Sulphur: The Life of Ibn Arabi,* trans. Peter Kingsley (Cambridge: Islamic Texts Society, 1993).

Adriel, Jean, *Avatar* (Santa Barbara, CA: J. F. Rowny Press, 1947).

Aftab, Tahera, *Inscribing South Asian Muslim Women: An Annotated Bibliography and Research Guide* (Leiden: Brill, 2008).

Ansari, Mhd Abdul Haq, *Sufism and Shariah: A Study of Shaykh Ahmad Sirhindi's Effort to Reform Sufism* (Leicester: Islamic Foundation, 1986).

Arberry, A. J., *Discourses of Rumi* (London: John Murray, 1961).

Arberry, A. J., trans., *Muslim saints and Mystics: Episodes from the Tadhkirat al- Auliya by Farid al-Din Attar* (London: Routledge and Kegan Paul, 1966).

Azadi, Siawosch, *Carpets in the Baluch Tradition* (Munich: Klinkhardt and Biermann, 1986).

Barfield, Thomas, *Afghanistan: A Cultural and Political History* (Princeton, NJ: Princeton University Press, 2010).

Bayly, C. A., *The New Cambridge History of India: Indian Society and the Making of the British Empire* (Cambridge, UK: Cambridge University Press, 1988).

Bernays, Robert, *Young India: Naked Faquir* (London, 1931; New York: H. Holt, 1932).

Birge, J. K., *The Bektashi Order of Dervishes* (London: Luzac, 1937).

Black, David, and Loveless, Clive, *Rugs of the Wandering Baluchi* (London: David Black, 1976).

Boucher, Jeff W., *Baluchi Woven Treasures* (revised edn, London: Laurence King, 1996).

Brodie, Fawn M., *The Devil Drives: A Life of Sir Richard Burton* (London: Eyre and Spottiswoode, 1967).

Bruijn, J. T. P. De, "The Qalandariyyat in Mystical Poetry, from Sanai Onwards" (75-86) in *The Legacy of Mediaeval Persian Sufism*, ed. Leonard Lewisohn (London: Khaniqahi Nimatullahi Publications, 1992).

Brunton, Paul, *A Search in Secret India* (London: Rider, 1934; second edn., 1970).

Buehler, Arthur F., *Sufi Heirs of the Prophet: The Indian Naqshbandiyya and the Rise of the Mediating Sufi Shaykh* (Columbia, SC: University of South Carolina Press, 1998).

------ *Revealed Grace: The Juristic Sufism of Ahmad Sirhindi* (Louisville, KY: Fons Vitae, 2011).

Burman, J. J. Roy, *Hindu-Muslim Syncretic Shrines and Communities* (New Delhi: Mittal Publications, 2002).

Burton, Richard F., *Sindh and the Races that Inhabit the Valley of the Indus* (London: W. H. Allen, 1851).

Caroe, Olaf, *The Pathans 550 B.C –A.D. 1957* (London: Macmillan, 1958).

Churchill, Winston, *The Story of the Malakand Field Force: An Episode of Frontier War* (London: Longmans, Green, 1898).

Cornell, Rkia E., ed. and trans., *Early Women Sufis: Dhikr an-niswa al-muta'abbidat as-sufiyyat* (Louisville, KY: Fons Vitae, 1999).

Deitrick, Ira G., ed. *Ramjoo's Diaries 1922-1929* (Walnut Creek, CA: Sufism Reoriented, 1979).

Eaton, Richard M., *Sufis of Bijapur 1300-1700: Social Roles of Sufis in Medieval India* (Princeton, NJ: Princeton University Press, 1978).

------ *The New Cambridge History of India: A Social History of the Deccan 1300-1761* (New York: Cambridge University Press, 2005).

Elias, Jamal J., *The Throne Carrier of God: The Life and Thought of Ala ad-dawla as- Simnani* (Albany, NY: State University of New York Press, 1995).

Elias, N., and Denison Ross, E., trans., *A History of the Moghuls of Central Asia: The Tarikh-i-Rashidi of Mirza Muhammad Haidar* (second edn, 1998; new impression, London: Curzon Press, 1972).

Ernst, Carl W., Eternal *Garden: Mysticism, History, and Politics at a South Asian Sufi* Center (Albany, NY: State University of New York Press, 1992).

------ and Bruce B. Lawrence, *Sufi Martyrs of Love: The Chishti Order in South Asia and Beyond* (New York: Palgrave, 2002).

Feldhaus, Anne, ed., *Images of Women in Maharashtrian Society* (Albany, NY: State University of New York Press, 1998).

Fischer, Louis, *The Life of Mahatma Gandhi* (London: Jonathan Cape, 1951).

Friedmann, Yohanan, *Shaykh Ahmad Sirhindi: An Outline of his Thought and a Study of his Image in the Eyes of Posterity* (Montreal: McGill-Queen's University Press, 1971).

Frye, Richard N., "Remarks on Baluchi History," *Central Asiatic Journal* (Wiesbaden 1961) 6: 44–50.

Ghani (Munsiff), Abdul "Hazrat Babajan of Poona" *Meher Baba Journal* (Feb. 1939) 1 (4): 29–39.

------ "Hazrat Baba Tajuddin of Nagpur," *Meher Baba Journal* (April 1939) 1 (6): 46–55.

Gordon, Stewart, *The New Cambridge History of India: The Marathas 1600-1818* (Cambridge and New York: Cambridge University Press, 1993).

Green, Nile, *Indian Sufism Since the Seventeenth Century: Saints, Books, and Empires in the Muslim Deccan* (New York: Routledge, 2006).

------ *Islam and the Army in Colonial India: Sepoy Religion and the Service of Empire* (New York: Cambridge University Press, 2009).

Grewal, J. S., *The New Cambridge History of India: The Sikhs of the Punjab* (Cambridge and New York: Cambridge University Press, 1991).

Haar, J. G. J. Ter, *Follower and Heir of the Prophet: Shaykh Ahmad Sirhindi (1564- 1624) as Mystic* (Leiden: Het Oosters Instituut, 1992).

Haeri, Muneera, *The Chishtis: A Living Light* (New York: Oxford University Press, 2000).

Hasrat, Bikrama Jit, *Dara Shikuh: Life and Works* (1953; second edn., New Delhi: Manoharlal, 1982).

Hasrat, Bikrama Jit, *Life and Times of Ranjit Singh: A Saga of Benevolent Despotism* (Punjab: Hathikhana, 1977);

Hazarah, Muhammad Khatib, The *History of Afghanistan – Fayz Muhammad Katib Hazarah's Siraj al-Tawarikh Vols I-3*, trans. R. D. McChesney and M. M. Khorrami, (Leiden: Brill, 2012).

James, Lawrence, *The Rise and Fall of the British Empire* (London: Little, Brown and Co., 1994).

James, Lawrence, *Raj: The Making and Unmaking of British India* (London: Little, Brown and Co., 1997).

Judson, Janet, ed., *Mehera* (New Jersey: Naosherwan Anzar, 1989).

Kalchuri, Bhau, *Lord Meher Vol. One* (North Myrtle Beach, SC: Manifestation, 1986).

------ *Lord Meher Vol. Two* (North Myrtle Beach, SC: Manifestation, 1987).

------ *Lord Meher Vol. Three* (North Myrtle Beach, SC: Manifestation, 1988).

Kantak, M. R., ed., *Hazrat Babajan: The Emperor of Spiritual Realm of her Time* (Poona: Meher Era Publications, 1981).

Karamustafa, Ahmet T., *God's Unruly Friends: Dervish Goups in the Islamic Later Middle Period, 1200-1550* (Salt Lake City, UT: University of Utah Press, 1994).

------ *Sufism: The Formative Period* (Edinburgh University Press, 2007).

Kaul, Chandrika, *From Empire to Independence: The British Raj in India 1858-1947* (BBC online article, 2011).

Kennedy, Dane, *The Highly Civilised Man: Richard Burton and the Victorian World* (Cambridge, MA: Harvard University Press, 2005).

Kotwal, Najoo Savak, *He Gives the Ocean: Stories of the Savak Kotwal Family's Life with Meher Baba* (Myrtle Beach, SC: Sheriar Foundation, 2006).

Kopruluzade, Mehmed Fuad, *Influence du Chamanisme Turco-Mongol sur les Ordres Mystiques Musulmans* (Istanbul: Imp. Zellitch Frères, Pera, Rue Yazidji, 1929).

Kruijtzer, Gijs, *Xenophobia in Seventeenth Century India* (Leiden: Leiden University Press, 2009).

Krynicki, Annie Krieger, *Captive Princess: Zebunnisa, Daughter of Emperor Aurangzeb*, trans. Enjum Hamid (New York: Oxford University Press, 2006).

Lapidus, Ira M., *A History of Islamic Societies* (Cambridge: Cambridge University Press, 1988).

Lawrence, Bruce B., *Notes from a Distant Flute: Sufi Literature in Pre-Mughal India* (Tehran: Imperial Iranian Academy of Philosophy, 1978).

------ "An Indo-Persian Perspective on the Significance of Early Persian Sufi Masters" (19–32) in *Classical Persian Sufism: From Its Origins to Rumi*, ed. Leonard Lewisohn (London: Khaniqahi Nimatullahi Publications, 1993).

------ and David Gilmartin, ed., *Beyond Turk and Hindu: Rethinking Religious Identities in Islamicate South Asia* (Gainesville, FL: University Press of Florida, 2000).

Longworth Dames, Mansel, *The Baloch Race: A Historical and Ethnological Sketch* (London: Royal Asiatic Society, 1904).

Marek, Jan, "Persian Literature in India" (713–734) in *History of Iranian* Literature, J. Rypka et al., (Dordrecht: Reidel, 1968).

Masson, Charles, *Narrative of various journeys in Balochistan, Afghanistan, and the Punjab* (4 vols, London: Richard Bentley, 1842-44).

Masson, Jeffrey, *My Father's Guru: A Journey Through Spirituality and Disillusion* (London: Harper Collins, 1993).

Mills, James H., *Cannabis Britannica: Empire, Trade, and Prohibition 1800-1928* (New York: Oxford University Press, 2003).

Moon, Penderel, *The British Conquest and Domination of India* (2 vols, London: Gerald Duckworth, 1989).

Mujeeb, M., *The Indian Muslims* (London: George Allen and Unwin, 1967).

Nicholson, Reynold A., trans., *Kashf al-Mahjub of Al Hujwiri: The Oldest Persian Treatise on Sufism* (1911; new edn, London: Luzac, 1936).

Nurbakhsh, Javad, *Masters of the Path: A History of the Nimatullahi Sufi Order* (New York: Khaniqahi Nimatullahi Publications, 1980).

Purdom, Charles B., *The Perfect Master* (London: Williams and Norgate, 1937).

------ *The God-Man: The Life, Journeys, and Work of Meher Baba with an interpretation of his silence and spiritual teaching* (London: George Allen and Unwin, 1964).

Raffiudin Ahmed, *History of the Baloch Regiment 1820-1939* (Abbotabad, Pakistan: Baluch Regimental Centre, 1998).

Rice, Edward, *Captain Sir Richard Francis Burton: A Biography* (New York: Scribner's, 1990).

Richards, John F., *The New Cambridge History of India: The Mughal Empire* (Cambridge: Cambridge University Press, 1993).

Rizvi, Saiyid Athar Abbas, *Muslim Revivalist Movements in Northern India in the 16th and 17th Centuries* (Agra University, 1965).

------ *Religious and Intellectual History of the Muslims in Akbar's Reign* (New Delhi: Manoharlal, 1975).

------ *A History of Sufism in India* (2 vols, New Delhi: Manoharlal, 1978–83).

Schimmel, Annemarie, *Mystical Dimensions of Islam* (Chapel Hill: University of North Carolina Press, 1975).

------ *Islam in the Indian Subcontinent* (Leiden: E. J. Brill, 1980).

------The *Triumphal Sun: A Study of the Works of Jalaloddin Rumi* (Albany, NY: State University of New York Press, 1993).

Schloss, Malcolm, "Thus Have I Heard," *The Awakener* (New York, 1966) 11 (1):1–5.

Shepherd, Kevin R. D., *A Sufi Matriarch: Hazrat Babajan* (Cambridge: Anthropographia, 1986).

-------*Gurus Rediscovered: Biographies of Sai Baba of Shirdi and Upasni Maharaj of Sakori* (Cambridge: Anthropographia, 1986).

------ *From Oppression to Freedom: A Study of the Kaivani Gnostics* (Cambridge: Anthropographia, 1988).

------- *Meher Baba, an Iranian Liberal* (Cambridge: Anthropographia, 1988).

------ *Minds and Sociocultures Vol One: Zoroastrianism and the Indian Religions* (Cambridge: Philosophical Press, 1995).

------ *Some Philosophical Critiques and Appraisals* (Dorchester, Dorset: Citizen Initiative, 2004).

------- *Investigating the Sai Baba Movement: A Clarification of Misrepresented Saints and Opportunism* (Dorchester, Dorset: Citizen Initiative, 2005).

------- *The Life of Meher Baba* (unpublished manuscript).

------- "Hazrat Babajan, A Pathan (Pashtun) Sufi." Accessed September 10, 2013. www.kevinrdshepherd. info/hazrat_babajan.html

------- "Meher Baba and Paul Brunton." Accessed September 10, 2013. www.citizenthought.net/Meher_Baba_and_ Paul_Brunton.html

------- "Sheriar Mundegar Irani and Zoroastrianism." Accessed September 10, 2013. www. independentphilosophy.net/Sheriar_Mundegar_Irani. html

------- "Shirdi Sai Baba and the Sai Baba Movement." Accessed September 10, 2013. www.kevinrdshepherd. info/shirdi_sai_baba_and_sai_baba_movement.html

Singh, Khushwant, *A History of the Sikhs Vols 1 and 2*, second edn. (OUP India: Oxford University Press, 2004–5).

Singh, Khushwant, *A History of the Sikhs Vol. 1: 1469-1839*, first edn. (Princeton University Press, 1963), pp. 196ff.

Singh, Patwant, *Empire of the Sikhs: The Life and Times of Maharaja Ranjit Singh* (London: Peter Owen, 2008).

Smith, Margaret, *Rabi'a the mystic and her fellow-saints in Islam* (Cambridge University Press, 1928; repr. Amsterdam: Philo Press, 1974),

Spear, Percival, *A History of India Vol. 2* (Harmondsworth: Penguin, 1970).

Stevens, Don. E., ed., *Listen Humanity* (New York: Dodd, Mead, 1957).

Subhan, John A., *Sufism, Its Saints and Shrines* (1938; repr. New York: Samuel Weiser, 1970).

Trimingham, J. Spencer, *The Sufi Orders in Islam* (Oxford: Oxford University Press, 1971).

Warren, Marianne, *Unravelling the Enigma: Shirdi Sai Baba in the Light of Sufism* (New Delhi: Sterling Publishers, 1999).

Wilson, Peter L., and Pourjavardy, Nasrollah, *Kings of Love: The Poetry and History of the Ni'matullahi Sufi Order* (Tehran: Imperial Iranian Academy of Philosophy, 1976).

Zebunnisa, *The Diwan of Zeb-Un-Nissa* , trans. M. Lal and J. D. Westbrook (London: John Murray, 1913).

Index